A Scholar's Odyssey

SBL
Society of Biblical Literature
Biblical Scholarship in North America

Number 20
A Scholar's Odyssey

Cyrus H. Gordon

Cyrus H. Gordon

A Scholar's Odyssey

Society of Biblical Literature
Atlanta, Georgia

A Scholar's Odyssey

Cyrus H. Gordon

Copyright © 2000 by the Society of Biblical Literature

All rights reserved. No part of this work may be reproduced or transmitted in any form or by any means, electronic or mechanical, including photocopying and recording, or by means of any information storage or retrieval system, except as may be expressly permitted by the 1976 Copyright Act or in writing from the publisher. Requests for permission should be addressed in writing to the Rights and Permissions Office, Society of Biblical Literature, 825 Houston Mill Road, Atlanta, GA 30329 USA.

Library of Congress Cataloging-in-Publication Data

Gordon, Cyrus Herzl, 1908–
    A scholar's odyssey / Cyrus H. Gordon.
        p. cm. — (Biblical scholarship in North America ; no. 20)
    Includes bibliographical references and index.
    ISBN 0-88414-016-4 (alk. paper)
       1. Gordon, Cyrus Herzl, 1908– 2. Biblical scholars—United States—Biography. I. Title. II. Series.

BS1161.G67 A3 2000
930'.07'202—dc21
[B]   99-086131

08 07 06 05 04 03 02 01 00   5 4 3 2 1

Printed in the United States of America
on acid-free paper

To my parents, Benjamin and Dorothy Gordon,
who gave me not only life but also my way of life.

TABLE OF CONTENTS

Acknowledgements ix
Introduction 1
1. Heritage 5
2. Education 13
3. Beginning a Career 21
4. Early Teaching Career 53
5. World War II 61
6. Tenure at Last! 79
7. Retirement 105
Ongoing Research 107
Appendix A: List of Doctoral Students 113
Appendix B: Bibliography of Works
    Ancient Near East: History and Institutions 119
    Aramaic–Syriac–Mandaic Studies 120
    Art and Archaeology of the Near East 122
    Assyriology 123
    Biblical Studies 124
    Comparative Literature and Linguistics 129
    Current Affairs 131
    Dead Sea Scrolls 131
    Ebla 131
    Egypto-Semitic Studies 133
    General Semitic Studies 134

Hebrew Language	135
Judaic Miscellanea	136
Long-Range Diffusion	136
Mediterranean Studies	138
Miscellaneous	138
Minoan	138
Nuzi	141
Phoenician and Hebrew Inscriptions	142
Scripts and Their Decipherment	142
Ugarit	143
Index	147

ACKNOWLEDGEMENTS

I am beholden to Thomas Olbricht for reading my manuscript and making many valuable suggestions pertaining to sequence and format. My style is admittedly elliptical and I tend to assume too much technical knowledge on the part of many of my readers. Dr. Olbricht has improved my presentation by getting me to fill in many gaps in the prefinal draft. He also tracked down biographical data for many of the people I mention.

Thanks are also due to Kent Richards for his enthusiasm and effort in bringing this book to publication.

Above all, I am heavily indebted to my wife Connie for her practical help. I can never thank her enough for her contributions.

INTRODUCTION

In this autobiographical sketch I intend to summarize the various facets of my contributions, show their interrelationships, provide a self-evaluation of them, and indicate where they may lead us in the decades to come. I do so out of concern lest my legacy become fragmented and that, in the process, some of its most significant parts become lost in the shuffle.

This autobiography does not deal with psychological hang-ups, my love life, or *Weltschmerz*. I refer readers interested in psychological hang-ups to the *Confessions* of Jean-Jacques Rousseau, and in sex-life to the memoirs of Casanova. I cannot compete with them as a psychological mess or as a great lover whose innumerable nights with Venus were followed by years with Mercury. My "autobiography" is rather a scholar's account of his professional life and work.

That is not to say, however, that this work consists entirely of a catalogue of degrees earned, archaeological expeditions completed, courses taught, and books written. In fact, the anecdotal parts of my autobiography will often be of greatest interest to students and scholars alike. In general, what I have observed in real life is more authentic than what I have read in books.

I was privileged to embark on Mediterranean and Near East studies while rather young and received my Ph.D. in June 1930, shortly before my twenty-second birthday. As a result, I became personally acquainted with a number of savants who have made seminal contributions and become legendary among several generations of scholars younger than I. My personal experiences with these giants oftentimes shed new light on their numerous accomplishments, to which we remain indebted.

My early years were conventional; my schooling, old-fashioned. I went to an eminently solid Ivy League University for my undergraduate and doctoral training. My teachers included a number of pillars of scholarship, while the curriculum I completed was conservative, embracing as it did Hebrew, Greek, and Latin. Yet even within this context I instinctively associated interrelated facts where previous scholars had sensed no relationship. Little did I realize that my mode of thinking would eventually make of me a disturber of the *pax academica* and eventually broaden my work from specialized aspects of philology to global diffusion.

Gradually I came to view worldwide humanity as a unit, with mobility at work to such a degree that none of us are aborigines in whatever land we call our own. Because humankind—and particularly civilized humankind—is composed of interrelated segments, no group of people has arisen in isolation from the rest of humanity. We are, in reality, all members of one family. But until we recognize this, there can be no foundation on which to build global peace. I do not mean to imply that such an awareness will automatically solve every menacing problem, only that without it those problems cannot and will not be solved.

During the cold war, scientists had a duty to do all that they could to ward off the destruction of the human race by nuclear atomic irresponsibility. Now that the cold war is over, the humanist must shoulder the duty of laying the foundation for promoting global peace.

As we acquire increased insight into past peoples and civilizations, the interlacing of all that precedes us becomes more and more obvious. We can, at last, conceive of a global world history. The story of my life is the quest to accomplish that task, though I know it is unattainable in my lifetime. Yet the wisdom of Rabbi Tarfon describes what animates me: "It is not incumbent on you to finish the task, but neither are you free to desist therefrom" (*m. ʾAbot* 2:1). The realization that I will not reach this goal does not frustrate me. On the contrary, I gratefully embrace it, for as long as I am alive I want to keep working, to keep approaching my goal. I do not wish to reach the end of the road, for then the remainder of my life would cease to have an ever-growing meaning.

Now, at the age of ninety-one, I recognize why my career has been fraught with pain yet crowned with satisfactions that scholars who live by conformity and compromise can never know. I sought the truth wherever I found it and followed it wherever it led me. My professional life has been long on naiveté and short on the "political correctness" that prevails in the halls of academe. Indeed, well-meaning and well-disposed members of the Establishment often advised me to join the mainstream. But their counsel was of no avail. I was driven from within to swim upstream. I served the cause of truth as I saw it, without counting the cost.

In the midst of this struggle and search for the truth, however, I have also enjoyed a lighter side to my life and career. There is, in fact, a human comedy as well as a human tragedy constantly unfolding before our eyes, and we can usually choose which show we will watch. My favorite hobby is observing the human comedy. It is going on all around us, and unlike the movies, one does not have to buy a ticket to see the performance.

Academia, for example, puts on stage a fair number of pompous buffoons whose antics often border on comedy. These individuals fit well Albert Einstein's comment regarding a prestigious university campus, "I have never seen so many pygmies on stilts." I must admit that I am frequently amused at the familiar sight of mediocrities trying to act like geniuses.

Introduction

A true genius such as Einstein, however, feels no need to sound his or her own horn. I had the good fortune to meet Albert Einstein during my years at Dropsie College (1946–1956). I lived in Princeton, and it happened that Edwin Samuel (the son of Sir Herbert Samuel), a visiting professor at Dropsie for a semester during that period, asked me to arrange a meeting with Einstein in Princeton. I did, and we drove to the Institute for Advanced Study, where we found Einstein waiting for us in his modest office.

During our meeting, Samuel asked Einstein how it felt to be hailed as the greatest man in the world. Einstein replied, "I have been lucky to have had a few good ideas, which have brought me fame. But those ideas are only a tiny part of me. The rest of me is ordinary, no better than the average truck driver or factory worker." This was not false modesty. Einstein knew he had ushered in the modern concept of the universe, supplanting Newton's system. But he was in most matters a simple soul, and he recognized that. Einstein was no pigmy on stilts.

I trust that the same might be said of me. I take no credit for all that I have accomplished. I believe that my background predetermined the shape and the direction of my career. As Yohanan ben Zakkai declared, "If you have attained considerable scholarship, do not take personal credit, because you were created for just that" (*m. ʾAbot* 2:9). I have sought to live by this assumption, as I hope this autobiography will reveal.

1.
HERITAGE

My parents were of more homogeneous background than couples in this age of romantic marriage and frequent divorce. In those days the parents of a prospective bride and groom typically investigated the two families carefully to make sure that the two sides were compatible. The community understood that a wedding does more than unite two individuals; it bonds two extended families. The couple, of course, if they found each other reasonably attractive, would give consent to the marriage, but the aim of wedlock was not so much sexual gratification or even companionship as the procreation and rearing of children to perpetuate a treasured way of life.

Both of my parents were Lithuanian Jews, members of a community that prized intellectual development. The Tsarist regime excluded Jews from the universities, but Jewish intellectualism flourished in the Talmudic academies for which Lithuania was justly famous.

The Talmud itself favors dialogue over dogma. The opinions of one sage, such as Hillel, are regularly pitted against those of another, such as Shammai. This dialogical approach created a climate conducive to intellectual growth in the academies. Although Hillel's milder opinions were generally preferred by the majority, Shammai's more stern minority opinions were accorded equal respect.

Moreover, although these Talmudic dialogues often entailed hair-splitting distinctions that seem trivial to modern scholars, they sharpened the mind and prepared Eastern European Jewish scholars to become an intellectual elite within western Christendom (which they did, especially from the 1920s to the 1970s). Eventually Lithuania's proximity to Germany (it bordered East Prussia) and the Jewish awareness that something worthwhile was taking place in the German universities, such as the one at Tilsit, helped pave the way for Jewish scholars to assume their place in the Arts and Sciences of the West.

I once asked Professor Harry Wolfson of Harvard University, a savant in ancient and medieval Greek as well as Jewish philosophy, how he evaluated the Greek mind, as exemplified by Aristotle, vis-à-vis the Talmudic mind. He replied: "If you compare a Greek philosophic treatise with a Talmudic tractate, obviously the Greek is orderly and easy to follow, whereas the rabbinic is disorderly and circuitous. But if you compare the 'mental horsepower' of the Greek philosopher and the rabbinic sage, the latter is superior." That was not the answer I expected, but eventually I realized that Wolfson was right.

In areas where one has convictions, there can be no real and constructive spirit of inquiry. For example, I am not interested in or open to modifying my firm loyalties (convictions), such as my feelings toward the United States or my ancestry. There may theoretically be better countries than mine, and there are certainly more distinguished family trees than mine, but this cannot alter my convictions (qua loyalties).

However, when dealing with issues of a scholarly nature, I regularly seek to understand both sides, taking each on its own terms without prejudice. For example, starting in my undergraduate days I studied the Arabic and Hebrew classics simultaneously but not comparatively. To show that either Judaism or Islam possessed *the truth* never crossed my mind. I felt comfortable in my tradition as an American Jew, but I simply would not assume that I had the ultimate truth (qua superiority) that eluded other people. I try not to offend "believers," whatever their truth might be, but I am instinctively faithful to my tradition of open inquiry and dialogical discovery, a tradition with strong roots in the Jewish communities of Lithuania.

My father, Benjamin L. Gordon (1870–1965) spent the first two decades of his life in his native land of Tsarist Lithuania. His home language was a local Yiddish dialect of German. The family name of "Gordon" is common among Jews of Lithuania and nearby areas, but it has not been modified from similar-sounding names such as "Gordonsky" or "Gordonovich," which, in any case, do not exist.

Several explanations have been proposed, but only one has any chance of being correct. It is known that Scottish people by the name of Gordon came as mercenaries to continental Europe. The *Encyclopaedia Britannica* reports that one of them, Patrick Gordon (b. 1635 in Scotland, d. 1699 in Moscow), went to continental Europe and served as a mercenary in the Polish-Swedish war of 1655–1660 (Micropaedia, vol. IV, 1978, p. 535). Gordon later became a favorite of Tsar Peter I (the Great), who made Gordon a rear admiral (1594) and chief military counselor.

Now, adventurers such as Patrick Gordon did not take their wives along with them but took up with local women. Of course, in modern Judaism, the children of any union are automatically Jewish if their mothers are Jewish. However, use of the father's name as the family name helped the Tsars keep track of their subjects for taxation and for military conscription. There must have been other adventuresome Gordons besides Patrick to account for the large number of Jewish Gordons from continental Europe.

At any rate, children in the Jewish communities of Lithuania began school at the age of three or four. Their curriculum included no secular subjects, and Hebrew was the only script used. The text that children studied first was the Pentateuch, starting with Genesis 1:1.

My father began his education in such a setting and continued his Hebraic studies until 1889, when he surreptitiously crossed the border under cover of darkness and, with the aid of an organized underground, reached the Atlantic port of Hamburg, Germany. There he boarded a ship for far-off "America the Golden." My father describes life as he experienced it in the Old World and in the New in his autobiography, *Between Two Worlds*.

The community my father left behind maintained rich ideals within a setting of material poverty. I shall cite only a single illustration to convey at least an inkling of that by-gone world, which was wiped out by the Holocaust. Students in the Talmudic academies were so indigent that the more affluent members of the community would donate the cost of as many meals as they felt they could afford. A philanthropic individual would tell the headmaster of a local academy that he was donating a specified number of student-meals per week, and the headmaster would then allocate the meals. Three square meals per day, seven days a week, if ever attained, would be striking it rich. My father told me that many was the time he had to subsist for a whole day on one meal. But intensive study, starting early in the morning and lasting into the night, was the main concern, and he had to go on no matter under what circumstances.

That system of education was hardly liberal, but it did teach students how to read and analyze a text. In raising my family, I subconsciously incorporated some of the same principles into it, as the following paragraphs will reveal.

My first wife, Joan, was very family oriented. She wanted to have a dozen children. But after our youngest (and hyperactive), Dan, was born in 1961, she realized that she had strength enough only for the five we then had: Deborah, Sarah, Rachel, Noah, and Dan.

For my part, I took my roles as a husband and as a father seriously. I went to the office and limited my teaching to two days a week so that I could be at home the rest of the week to do research and writing. The evening meal was especially important at our house, for it was then that we were all together, talking with and learning from one another.

Before our second child learned to walk and talk, I spent significant time with our oldest, Deborah, teaching her to read hieroglyphs and to translate simple Egyptian texts. When Deborah was about three years old, I took her one afternoon to the Metropolitan Museum in New York. We went to the Egyptian section, where I carried her along so she could see what was in the cases. Each object was labeled and listed the name of a particular pharaoh in hieroglyphs and in English. Some tourists standing nearby remarked to me how impressed they were with my child, who already knew her ABCs. Needless to say, they were stunned when I told them that Deborah did not know her ABCs but was reading the pharaonic names from the hieroglyphs.

Our family often discussed biblical and archaeological matters over dinner. But I made a point of being careful never to tell the children anything they might someday have to unlearn. One evening Deborah, when she was about eight, surprised me by asking, "Did Noah really build the ark? Did he really take pairs of animals aboard?" Before I had time to reply, Sarah, then about six, blurted out, "Whether or not Noah really built the ark is not important. The important thing is that you have to know the text!" Her remark not only conveys an idea of some of our table talk but also displays the importance that I placed on being able to read and analyze a text.

My father also valued the ability to read and analyze a text. Shortly after arriving in America with no knowledge of English, he inquired as to the best author of English literature. On learning that it was Shakespeare, he read all of Shakespeare's plays and went to see those that happened to be produced in Philadelphia during the 1890s. All the while he eked out a meager livelihood working as a librarian of Hebraica and Judaica and by giving private Hebrew lessons to Jewish children. He enhanced his modest income by qualifying as a ritual slaughterer, a task for which he had to pass a rabbinical examination on the Talmudic and other traditional regulations.

Still, my father wanted more. For centuries, the practice of medicine had an honored place among Hebrew scholars. Maimonides, the greatest of the great Jewish philosophers (1135–1204), was not only steeped in Hebraica and Judaica but earned his living as a famous physician, serving as the personal and court doctor of the Sultan of Egypt. Moreover, he wrote medical treatises in Arabic so that they were accessible to the Sultan. My father wanted to follow in Maimonides' footsteps.

The entrance requirements to the American medical schools in the 1890s were not up to today's standards. Yet they posed problems for my father, who did not know English well enough to understand the lectures. Undaunted, he worked to improve his English even while he attended a college preparatory school to learn enough Latin that he could at least begin to cope with medical terminology. He also had to take enough mathematics and science to qualify for the Jefferson Medical School in Philadelphia.

Eventually my father graduated with an M.D. degree in 1896, in large part because the Talmudic academies had taught him how to read, analyze, and understand a text. Gray's *Anatomy* may have introduced him to an entirely new world of knowledge, but understanding that text required significantly less "mental horsepower" than a page of Talmudic *pilpûl* (hairsplitting). The young man who had disembarked in Philadelphia in 1889, impecunious and unable to understand English, was now, only seven years later, an American Doctor of Medicine. The streets of America may not have been literally paved with gold, but my father's experience explains his fondness for "America the Golden."

My father had felt no patriotism toward the oppressive Tsarist Empire and had done all that he could to evade military service there. However, in 1898, as soon as the Spanish-American War broke out, he joined the U.S. Army, only to be disappointed that the war ended too quickly for him to see action. As a veteran, my father wore his uniform proudly on patriotic celebrations. Teddy Roosevelt was his ideal American leader. Needless to say, I was raised as a flag-waving American. Our family had no time for unpatriotic "isms" such as socialism or communism, let alone for the bomb-throwing anarchy movement and its many devotees, including the notorious Emma Goldman (1869–1940). Consequently, from childhood and through college, my friends, all from the intelligentsia, liked me personally but considered my patriotic values as holdovers from the age of the dinosaurs.

My parents never once told me that I had to study and become a scholar. Commands to that effect were unnecessary. Their hopes in me permeated our home, and I simply did my best to become a scholar. When I rebelled, it was not against the family's values, but against accepting the consensus simply because it was "politically correct." That kind of rebellion was considered a virtue and was even expected of bright children.

This "saving grace of heresy" had a place in our tradition, but it was to be expressed only in scholarly company. My paternal grandfather used to wait until his wife and children were asleep, whereupon he would kindle a lamp in order to read secular books. Officially, all secular reading was taboo, but for a Lithuanian intellectual the saving grace of heresy was an essential part of life.

Among common, unsophisticated members of the community, however, scholars were to blend in without disturbing their traditions. In fact, tradition was so crucial that, before children learned the alphabet, they were initiated into the tradition through rituals such as blessing (in Hebrew) and lighting the Sabbath candles. Such rituals, although the province of the often less-learned mother rather than of the more-educated father, were of vital importance for the survival of that way of life.

My own mother, Dorothy Cohen Gordon (1880–1955), came from Kovna, modern Kaunas. Her father's original family name was Kass, but he told the immigration official at Ellis Island that he would prefer a typical American name. The official suggested Cohen, which my grandfather did not recognize because Cohen was pronounced "kayhen" or "cain" in his dialect of Yiddish. So, although he was not of a priestly family, my maternal grandfather entered this country as "Mr. Cohen."

My mother was about nine years old when she entered New York City. In the old country she had attended a public school, where she had learned some Russian and French. She soon forgot these languages, but when I was a child she often lulled me to sleep with Russian and French songs. Her family was not intellectual per se, but, as was customary in Jewish families, my mother attended grammar school and took piano lessons—boys took violin. I recall her playing the piano softly as I fell asleep.

My grandfather was a successful businessman, owner of a clothing factory, what some might have called a "sweat shop." His son Sam eventually gave the factory to the workers. With his savings my grandfather purchased a number of small dwellings, which he fixed up and rented out. Although my mother's family was not intellectual, they revered scholarship, which explains why she married a man of my father's learning. At the same time, her father was able to give my father several houses as a dowry.

In the family thus formed, I enjoyed the companionship of three siblings: a sister, Judith (1904–1988); a younger brother, Norman (b. December 3, 1910); and my "baby" brother, Maurice (b. July 8, 1916). My mother was kept quite busy taking care of the house, the other children, and my father's office, so to a great extent I raised Maurice, who eventually became a physician. Maurice and I remained close and always kept in contact, notably in correspondence when I was abroad as a field archaeologist (1931–1935). Norman, Maurice, and I cherish our friendship, which has only increased over the years. I enjoy my relations with my brothers, their wives, and all my nephews and nieces.

My mother exerted a strong influence on me in many ways. She felt that anything worth doing had to be done right in every detail. This was, in fact, an important corrective to my father's approach to scholarship, which was less meticulous than what her uncompromising principles required. She was also critical of my father's practice of quoting other writers. She thought that a scholar's writings should be based on his or her own ideas, without repeating what others had written. I may not agree with my mother in every detail, but I must attribute my strong preference for primary over secondary sources and, above all, my emphasis on originality to her teachings during my formative years.

My mother had attended public school in New York during the 1890s and adhered to the Victorian values of those times. So, whenever I did anything incorrectly, she never expressed sympathy; rather, she told me to try harder. I am naturally left-handed, but my mother insisted that I write with my right hand, that I eat with my right hand, that I extend my right hand for shaking hands, and so on. I am also prone to making transpositions in spelling and the like. In those days there were no therapists for correcting such disabilities that we know as dyslexia. I simply followed my mother's instructions to try harder. All in all I think I have not done too badly.

In sum, the cardinal sin in our Lithuanian Jewish tradition was not heresy but ignorance. Anyone who preferred ignorance to knowledge was scorned as a benighted vulgarian. In the *shûl* (Yiddish for "school"), scholars not only studied apart from the common people but generally even prayed separately. They held a fantasy that in the afterlife, there is an Academy on high reserved for scholars alone. To translate this into modern terms: one has to become a scholar in this world (the Academy below) as an entrance requirement to the Academy on high. There are no remedial programs post mortem. This life is one's only chance to make the grade. Pious farmers, herdsmen, and artisans can go to heaven, but not as first-class citizens of the Academy on high. Such fantasies may be irrational, but they reflect the ideals of the community more vividly than many a scholarly tome on sociology, anthropology, or history.

2.
EDUCATION

My life-work was laid out for me before I entered grade school. Consequently, I never reached a fork in the road where I did not know whether to bear to the right or to the left. I knew the correct course to take and, unlike more "practical" people, I lived without compromise.

Public and Jewish Schools
In grade school, I learned the three Rs: reading, 'riting, and 'rithmetic, but the curriculum provided me with no intellectual stimulation. The teachers either hated me or favored me. Two of them skipped me ahead, each by one semester, which saved me a full year in grade school. Others, however, passed me with low grades. Apparently a few liked pupils with inquiring minds, but most preferred docile, unquestioning students.

My few friends at school came from the affluent, educated families on Broad Street. My family lived in the brownstone house at the northwest corner of Broad and Mifflin Streets, opposite the Saint Agnes Hospital, where my father was a staff physician. The bulk of my classmates were the children of illiterate Neapolitan and Sicilian families or African Americans descended from slaves who had been freed by the Civil War a mere half century earlier.

In general, the Jewish tradition of literacy and their reverence for scholarship taught them "what to do with a book." All of this gave them a decided initial advantage over some of the other ethnic groups. As a result, these groups did not early on produce college graduates, doctors, lawyers, judges, senators, and governors as quickly as the Jews. My Italian classmates came, not from the educated upper classes in the tradition of the Renaissance, but from poor, unschooled laborers who needed time to discover, and benefit from, the opportunities that America afforded to improve one's social status. Eventually, however, education enabled every one to overcome his initial disadvantages.

With one notable exception, I got along well with the different ethnic groups in the community. Because I was Jewish, the Italian gangs would attack me on my way home from school. To help me survive, my friend, Andy Callahan, the son of my Broad Street neighbor and Scotch-Irish physician named Dr. Andrew Callahan Sr., taught me how to fight. Then, when he felt I was ready, he would get the gang members to pick their champion for a fair one-to-one fight with me. Rare was the day when I came home from school unbloodied, but I learned how to fight. Those years did not scar me psychologically because I had unmitigated contempt for my assailants and was thankful for being who I was, and not like them.

In retrospect, I have often thought that my parents should have known better than to reside in such a neighborhood. But apparently they reckoned that living on Broad Street in a brownstone house uplifted the entire family, including the children. It was doubtless much better than anything my father or mother had experienced in Tsarist Lithuania. At any rate, we lived there from the time I was five until I turned twelve, when we moved to an almost suburban neighborhood in West Philadelphia with a more congenial mix of residents.

When I was about five years old, my father joined the congregation of Mikveh Israel, an old aristocratic synagogue of the Spanish and Portuguese tradition. Its past members included Haym Salomon (1740–1785), who had placed his fortune at George Washington's disposal to wage the War of Independence. Washington's letter to the Congregation was a prized treasure, a fact of which I became aware early on. My father's choice of synagogue was wise and foresighted. He chose not to affiliate himself with East European congregations because they maintained the Old World ways instead of assimilating to American ways. The German synagogues, on the other hand, were Americanized but, in those days, minimized Hebrew tradition, language, literature, and culture. By choosing Mikveh Israel, my father was able to maintain the traditions important to him while also adapting to a more American way of life.

Mikveh Israel offered a school for children that met on Sunday mornings and two weekdays after public school hours. There I received instruction in biblical Hebrew and Jewish history, and learned to sing parts of the Mikveh Israel liturgy. The curriculum was strong on Jewish tradition, but without dogma or any trace of fundamentalism. No invidious comparisons were made with other religions or with other branches of Judaism.

Upon completing the Mikveh Israel School for Observation and Practice in 1923, I continued my Hebraic and Judaic studies at Gratz College, founded in 1895 by Jewish leaders in Philadelphia. Although I had technically changed schools, I did not have to change locations, for Gratz College classes met in Mikveh Israel's buildings during the evenings. The college curriculum included advanced Hebrew grammar, some Talmud, and a full sweep of Jewish history. In 1926 I was awarded the diploma certifying me as a teacher of Hebraica and Judaica. Many years later I was delighted when, on June 2, 1996, at the centennial celebration of the college, Gratz conferred on me the honorary degree of Doctor of Hebrew Laws.

Among the leading longtime families of Mikveh Israel were the Solis-Cohens, who were not only prominent Philadelphia Jews but also ranked socially among Philadelphia's aristocracy. Both Jay and Solomon Solis-Cohen were professors at the Jefferson Medical School. Jay was the father of otolaryngology in America as well as a talented painter of urban architecture. His brother Solomon was both a respected internist and the English translator of medieval Spanish-Hebrew poetry for the Schiff Classics Series.

The enlightened atmosphere of Mikveh Israel instilled in me a feeling that the best of Judaism and the best of America were, in fact, identical. I subconsciously turned a blind eye to the very existence of Jewish fundamentalists. It was only years later when I was a professor that I faced the unpleasant fact that Jews (like non-Jews) had their full share of fundamentalists and various forms of "wild life." Still, my late awakening had a worthwhile side: I had grown up happy about my place in the world, without a scintilla of identity crisis.

I can also trace some of my basic attitudes toward scholarship to an early age. When I was about seven years old I took a long walk with a learned scholar named Professor Jacob Hoshander. He must have been a naive, sweet person because he treated me as an equal. He asked me if I had given thought to the Hebraic influence on Dante. Without waiting for a reply, he proceeded to recite from memory long passages in Hebrew and Italian. I understood very little of the Hebrew and not a word of the Italian, but I concealed my ignorance. His monologue simply created within me a desire to learn Dante's epics and their Hebraic background, whatever that might mean. Years later, as I prepared for an Italian sight-reading examination at the University of Pennsylvania, the memory of Hoshander impelled me to read many pages of Dante's immortal verses.

Even later still, when my mentor in graduate school, James A. Montgomery, suggested a topic for my doctoral dissertation, he said, "You are a Jewish scholar, and it takes a Jewish scholar to handle rabbinic sources such as the Babylonian and Jerusalem Talmuds. I would like you to write on 'Rabbinic Exegesis in the Vulgate of Proverbs.'" There were a number of errors in Montgomery's estimate of the situation, the most serious of which was his assumption that I was familiar with the entire gamut of rabbinic literature. Instead of protesting my ignorance, however, I resolved to live up to his illusions. Needless to say, I knew a great deal more about rabbinic literature when I finished my dissertation than when I started it. As before with Hoshander, I regarded a lack of knowledge, not as a shameful deficiency, but as an opportunity to expand my learning and scholarship even further.

After completing public grade school in 1921, I entered the local high school: West Philadelphia High School for Boys. Our building was separated from that of the West Philadelphia High School for Girls by a paved open space that served as a playground during recess. The students from both schools played in this open space, but never simultaneously. Indeed, contact or socializing between the sexes was not permitted on the school grounds. The only "infractions" of that rule were surreptitious glances that passed through the windows, across the yard separating the two schools. I completed my high-school courses in three years and received my diploma in 1924.

University

In those days, high-school graduates were a small and respected minority. Even in upper middle-class neighborhoods in large metropolitan centers such as Philadelphia, only a small proportion of high-school graduates continued on to college. I, of course, did so. I applied for entrance to only one college: the University of Pennsylvania. Located in West Philadelphia, it was a mere twenty-minute ride by public transportation from my home.

The University of Pennsylvania offered an ideal setting for a nascent scholar such as myself. The University had an honored tradition in Near Eastern studies and numbered on its faculty scholars who could teach me the primary sources. The roots of Oriental studies had taken hold at the University of Pennsylvania in the 1880s. In the early part of the nineteenth century, the systematic study of the Hebrew Bible had flourished primarily in newly founded seminaries at Andover, Harvard, Yale, Princeton, and elsewhere. Since the University of Pennsylvania did not have a seminary, Oriental studies focused upon the languages and literature of the ancient Middle and Near East, an emphasis that was quite to my liking.[1]

My mentor, Professor James A. Montgomery, remains my ideal of a scholar and a gentleman.[2] Montgomery taught me, among other things, Syro-Aramaic dialects (including Mandaic) and Geez (Ethiopic). Although

---

[1] For additional background on the University of Pennsylvania, see my book, *The Pennsylvania Tradition of Semitics* (SBLCP; Atlanta: Scholars Press, 1986).

[2] Montgomery (1866–1949) was born in Philadelphia and educated at the University of Pennsylvania and the Philadelphia Divinity School. From 1890–1892, he, along with about three hundred other Americans, studied in Germany, since German universities were at the forefront in biblical Studies, ancient languages, church history, and theology. He served as professor of Hebrew at Philadelphia Divinity School from 1899 to 1935, and simultaneously at the University of Pennsylvania from 1909 to 1938. In 1909–1910 and 1913–1914 he was editor of the *Journal of Biblical Literature*. In 1918 he served as president of the Society of Biblical Literature. He was active in the American Schools of Oriental Research (ASOR), serving as director of the Jerusalem school (1914–1915) and as president (1921–1933). He published several works on Old Testament languages and history as well as commentaries.

my A.B., M.A., and Ph.D. were conferred after special comprehensive oral and written examinations, which included extensive outside reading lists, they really blended into each other. My M.A. thesis addressed the legal court procedures and terminology in the world of the Hebrew Bible, while my Ph.D. dissertation examined "Rabbinic Exegesis in the Vulgate of Proverbs." In reality, my doctorate was conferred only when I was ready to do independent research and to teach. Likewise, throughout my teaching career the central criterion by which I evaluated students was whether or not they were ready independently to perform and publish research and to teach"[3]

During my time at the University of Pennsylvania, I also took Akkadian with Ephraim Speiser. The courses were actually graduate courses but were open to undergraduates who could blend in. My official major for the first three semesters was mathematics. I believed that the discipline of mathematics—as well as the use of graphs, permutations and combinations, and the like—would give structure to my life's work. Yet I never lost sight of my ultimate goal, to become a scholar in Near Eastern studies.

During my Penn years, I also took courses at Dropsie College, though not for credit. Professor Max Margolis's courses at Dropsie focused mainly on OT Hebrew linguistics. They proved particularly helpful because they enabled me to compose my *Ugaritic Grammar* years later. I was also privileged to take courses on Arabic at Dropsie. Montgomery taught Arabic grammar at Penn, but his Christianity got in the way of his teaching of the Qur'an, and he often referred to Muhammad as "that imposter." I studied Arabic at Dropsie with Solomon Skoss, who described Muhammad more accurately as a great charismatic leader who changed the course of world history. Likewise at Dropsie, I studied Talmud with Solomon Zeitlin, a brilliant scholar whose unconventional ways and lack of standard training were more productive of originality than of soundness. When I asked him about his early grammar-school training, he replied, "I was a genius and did not need any."

At the University of Pennsylvania, George Aaron Barton taught a number of courses, including Sumerian.[4] Barton's chief merit was his readiness

---

[3] See Appendix A for a partial list of my doctoral students.

[4] Barton (1859–1942) was born in Quebec and received the B. A. from Haverford College in 1882. In 1891 he received the first Ph.D. awarded by Harvard in Semitics, with a dissertation titled "The Semitic Ishtar Cult." He was appointed a professor at Bryn Mawr. In 1902–1903 he served as the director of the American School of Oriental Research in Jerusalem. In 1921 he was the first director of the Baghdad School. In 1922 he was appointed professor of Semitic languages and the history of religion at the University of Pennsylvania, where he served until his retirement in 1932. He also taught at the Episcopal Divinity School in Philadelphia (1921–1937), where he was professor of New Testament religion and language.

to dive into any language, always in the original script. However, in those days (the early 1920s), cuneiform Hittite was a new subject for which Barton lacked the necessary Indo-European background. He jumped into it anyway, and the results were less than stellar. He also published Sumerian texts and gave courses on Sumerian in which Samuel Noah Kramer and I were the only students.[5] Interestingly enough, Barton's methods repelled Kramer and discouraged him from pursuing the language. Years later, however, when he was at the Oriental Institute of the University of Chicago, Kramer decided to study Sumerian with Arno Poebel, a great Sumerologist. When Poebel told him, "Unless you admit that all your previous education is worthless, I cannot accept you as a student," it was precisely the shock treatment that Kramer needed. He studied with Poebel for only a few months, but the experience was so intense that it proved to be the foundation on which Kramer's career as a famous Sumerologist was built.

Being able to read relevant secondary sources in modern European languages is valuable for research. Thus, I regret never learning the Slavonic languages and Hungarian. However, I was able to develop, over time, sight-reading facility in the Romance and Teutonic languages. To achieve this, I spent an hour each day of my 1929 summer vacation on each of six languages: French, Italian, Dutch, Portuguese, Spanish, and Dano-Norwegian. I had already developed fluency in reading, writing, and speaking German and Swedish, thanks to the tutelage of E. C. Wesselhoeft and Axel Johann Uppvall, respectively. While studying Swedish, I had realized that if one worked to understand every word and detail of grammar in the first twenty pages of a book, the rest of the book could be readily grasped. Each author has a distinctive style that, when mastered, carries the reader along.

When I began my summer project, I would rapidly work through a grammar book for each language and begin reading a volume of professional interest to me. I would look up in a dictionary every word that I did not know and write it on one side of a folded sheet of paper and the English translation on the other side. Then, when my daily hour of study was drawing to a close, I would read down the list of foreign words, checking off each when I remembered its meaning. When all the words were checked off, I would work through the list of English translations and check off each when I knew its foreign original. Finally, I would throw the folded sheet away. Saving word lists is of no value. The words must be in

---

[5] Samuel Kramer (1897–1990) was born near Kiev. His family came to Philadelphia in 1905. He received the B.S. from Temple University, and his studies at Dropsie ended in 1925. He completed a Ph.D. under Ephraim Speiser in 1929. In 1932 he took a position at the Oriental Institute of the University of Chicago. In 1948 he left Chicago to become professor of Assyriology at the University of Pennsylvania. He specialized in Sumerian documents and history.

our heads. If we have to learn a particular word again, so be it. Until it is in our heads, our job is not done. At any rate, as a result of my intensive study, I passed the sight-reading tests administered by the departments of modern languages at Penn before embarking on my doctoral program.

As I have already mentioned, Montgomery suggested that I write my doctoral dissertation on "Rabbinic Exegesis in the Vulgate of Proverbs." The idea was to track down interpretations that Jerome obtained from the Jewish teachers with whom he studied Hebrew in Palestine. Proverbs was chosen because it contains essentially secular wisdom and thus little or no Christian doctrine that might have shaped Jerome's interpretations. This approach sounds straightforward enough, but I also recognized that I could not attribute interpretations anticipated in the Septuagint, Vetus Latina, or similar sources to Jerome's Jewish informants. Since these works were available to Jerome's contemporaries—Christian scholars who were unacquainted with rabbinic literature—the interpretations within them could not be traced with any certainty to Jerome's Jewish teachers.

Consequently, I needed to work through these sources as well as the rabbinic literature before I would be able to point out the influence of his Jewish teachers. Jerome mentions one of his teachers by name: Bar Anina, which can only stand for Bar Ḥanina. Unfortunately, this name was far too common for us to identify Jerome's teacher with a particular Rabbi Bar Ḥanina. We do know that Jerome's contact with his Jewish teachers took place secretly at night. But the secret leaked out. When his Christian enemies accused him of studying Hebrew Scripture under the tutelage of Jews, he replied, "Peritis in arte sua credendum est" ("You have to depend on the experts in their own art"). Jerome recognized that the rabbis were the experts on the Hebrew language and Scriptures and that, in order to become expert himself, he needed to study with them.

Writing the dissertation obliged me to scrutinize a plethora of Greek, Latin, Aramaic, Hebrew, and other texts. This was good training for a young scholar. It also had a lasting effect on me. I became consciously dedicated to international and interconfessional cooperation in scholarship. Soon afterwards the Pontificium Institutum Biblicum in Rome invited me to contribute an article to the Festschrift in honor of Anton Deimel on the occasion of his seventieth birthday.[6] Deimel was a productive Sumerologist, as the continued usefulness of his *Šumerisches Lexikon* (seven quarto volumes) demonstrates. This invitation led to a long and

---

[6] Anton Deimel (1865–1954) was born in Olpe Westphalia. He entered the Society of Jesus in the Netherlands. He studied cuneiform with J. N. Strasmeier in London (1904–1907). With the founding of the Pontifical Biblical Institute in Rome in 1909, he became professor of Assyriology. He published Sumerian texts and lexica and founded *Orientalia* in 1920.

fruitful association with the P.I.B., which, under the forceful editorship of the late Alfredo Pohl, pursued a policy of welcoming sound scholarship regardless of an author's religion or nationality.[7]

While I was pursuing my earned degrees (A.B., M.A., Ph.D.) at the University of Pennsylvania (1924–1930), I also attended all the courses offered by Professor Max L. Margolis at The Dropsie College in Philadelphia.[8] I did not need, nor did I take, academic credit for those courses. I took them because Margolis was the most thorough scholar I have ever known. As I previously mentioned, Margolis taught me the ins and outs of Semitic linguistics, which enabled me to compose my *Ugaritic Grammar* in 1940. Years later, Édouard Dhorme noted that I had entered the Ugaritic field when it was chaotic, with everyone feeling free to interpret as he or she pleased, and that I had formulated the rules of the language that have stood the test of time and dispelled the chaos. Until Dhorme wrote this in a letter to me, I had not fully realized the achievement inherent in my *Ugaritic Grammar*. But one thing I did recognize: although Margolis never worked with Ugaritic nor mentioned Ugarit to me, it was his instruction that drummed in the facts and principles that enabled me not only to write a Ugaritic grammar but to take my place in the broader scholarly community.

---

[7] Alfredo Pohl (1890–1961) was born in Koebernitz, Upper Silesia. He entered the Society of Jesus in 1912. He studied Assyriology with Bruno Meisner from 1924 to 1930. He became Professor of Assyriology and Oriental history at the Pontifical Biblical Institute Rome in 1930. He published Sumerian and Babylonian texts, and edited *Analecta Orientalia*.

[8] Margolis (1866–1932) was the most important Jewish biblical scholar before World War I. He was born into a rabbinic family in Tsarist Lithuania. After studying in Berlin, he came to America and took a Ph.D. under Richard Gottheil (1862–1936) at Columbia University. Margolis taught at Hebrew Union College in Cincinnati from 1893 to 1897 and in 1909 became professor of biblical philology at The Dropsie College for Hebrew and Cognate Learning, the college itself having been organized in 1907. Margolis served as editor for the *Journal of Biblical Literature* (1914–1922) and was president of the Society of Biblical Literature in 1923.

3.
BEGINNING A CAREER

After receiving a Ph.D in June 1930, I spent the following academic year as an instructor of Hebrew and Akkadian at the University of Pennsylvania (1930–1931). Then, as throughout my career, I taught from texts in their original scripts. I read biblical Hebrew with undergraduates, Akkadian texts with graduate students. Zelig Harris, who later distinguished himself as a theoretical linguist and the mentor of Noam Chomsky, studied Hammurabi's Code with me.

With regard to teaching methods I emulated Max Margolis, though not in every way. Margolis was the best teacher I ever had, but he used shock treatment on his students in class. He would fire a half verse of the Hebrew Bible at a student. If the student could not tell in which book of the Bible it occurred, Margolis would bark at the student, "Go to hell!" If the next student could not locate it either, Margolis would say, "There's room for you there, too."

Young and full of self-confidence, I reacted by telling Margolis privately, "I am willing to go to hell for you, but it would be more fun if I knew the right answer more often. How can I achieve that?" "Tonight," he advised me, "start reading the Bible, beginning with Genesis 1:1. Continue this every evening until you come to the end of the Hebrew Bible at the close of 2 Chronicles. If you do not know a particular word, don't worry about it. If it is a common word, it will occur time and again. If it is a rare word, take comfort in the knowledge that no one knows the meaning of every word in the Bible." After several months, I had completed Margolis's assignment, so I informed him of as much and asked him what to do next. "Do it again!" he replied. Gradually I came to recognize more and more of the quotations he fired at me and eventually became a star student. Unfortunately, many of the other students were married men in their forties, all too aware that their careers were at stake. Some even suffered nervous breakdowns.

My personality was quite different from Margolis's. I never asked a student a question that he or she did not have inner resources to answer. Often a student would be too flustered to answer technical questions correctly, in which case I would ask the student to step up to the blackboard and write the word, even if it was incorrect. I then asked the student to apply Margolis's formulaic rules, which were listed on a sheet of paper. No student was asked to memorize the rules, only to apply them. After a few applications of the rules, I would instruct the student to refer to a biblical passage where the word occurs. I then showed how the correct answer was within reach, if only the student would play the game according to its rules.

My students came from various backgrounds and diverse religions. I was never interested in converting anyone, only in training everyone to use primary sources to get at the truth. Whether the truth was Coptic or Yemenite mattered not a bit. I also drew on the knowledge of my students to enrich the classes. I often had Jews, Christians, and Muslims all in the same class, and it was not uncommon for rabbis and Christian ministers to learn side by side. Some students knew their Scripture well, while some were Talmudists and scholars versed in other ancient sources. I had students knowledgeable in ancient art as well as those with background in the classical world, including languages and art. In order to avoid political and religious friction pertaining to modern affairs, I excluded all data after Napoleon. I take pride in the mutual respect and interest my students held for each other.

I frequently brought outside data into class discussions, but when they were critical of students, I always presented them with a smile. For example, I once related a story I had heard from the Zen Buddhist Professor Suzuki of Columbia University, a man I greatly admired. He mentioned the shock treatment of Zen Buddhist gurus. One disciple, after sitting at the feet of his guru for twenty years, asked, "What is god and where is he?" The teacher whipped out a decaying carrot and said, "This is god." When the student exclaimed, "I do not understand!" the guru replied, "Of course not. You are an idiot who has not achieved enlightenment after twenty years. There is another teacher two thousand miles away. I want you to walk to him; perhaps he will succeed in enlightening you." Well, the crestfallen disciple, after walking a thousand miles, saw a beautiful wildflower. He cried out, "God is everything and everywhere, be it the loveliest flower or a rotting carrot." So the disciple returned to his old master and thanked him for shocking him into enlightenment. At this point I turned to the class and, with a smile, asked, "Why can't I solve your problems simply by telling you to walk to another teacher in California?" I paused then answered, "Because in America we are not interested in enlightenment but in transfer credits."

Archaeology in the Middle and Near East

During my first year of teaching, James Montgomery, who was also President of the American Schools of Oriental Research in Jerusalem and Baghdad, urged me to accept a fellowship at the Baghdad School.[9] This

---

[9] The American School of Oriental Studies and Research was founded in 1900. Two other organizations paved the way for it, the Archaeological Institute of

would enable me to spend the winter season excavating in Iraqian Kurdistan simultaneously at the sites of Tepe Gawra and Tell Billa, and the summer season in southern Palestine excavating at the Maccabean fortress of Beth-Sur. I accepted, and the appointment turned out to last for four years (1931–1935).

As soon as I accepted, Montgomery informed me that, on my way to Baghdad, I should stop in Istanbul to study and to prepare for publication the collection of Aramaic magic bowls in the Museum of Antiquities located there. The bowls had been excavated by a University of Pennsylvania expedition at Nippur in southern Iraq, which then formed part of the Ottoman Empire. At that time the Sultan had presented about forty of the bowls to the University of Pennsylvania Museum, and Montgomery had studied and published them in a volume of Publications of the Babylonian Section of the University Museum. It was typical of Montgomery that, whenever he finished an opus, he did not dwell on it but shifted his attention to other proj-

---

America (1879) and the Society of Biblical Literature (1880). The first American dig in the Near East was at Nippur, a center of Sumerian culture, under the auspices of the University of Pennsylvania in 1888. It was particularly in meetings of the Society of Biblical Literature that certain important American scholars, J. Henry Thayer, for example, emphasized the need for an organization focused upon biblical archaeology. Through the encouragement of ASOR, several important scholars and universities had undertaken many important digs by 1930. The first and main center was opened in Jerusalem. The Baghdad branch of ASOR officially opened in 1923, with George A. Barton (1859–1942), a professor at Pennsylvania (1922–1932), as director.

The American practice of Near Eastern archaeology came into its own with ASOR's founding of a school in Jerusalem in 1900. British and continental groups had already been at work. Much of the work of these early years consisted of field trips to collect artifacts, mostly potsherds, by visiting several sites. Two principal developments led to modern "scientific archaeology." A first major step was taken by George A. Reisner (professor of Egyptology at Harvard, 1905–1942) and his architect, Clarence S. Fisher, in a 1910 excavation of Samaria. They worked out a systematic method for debris-layer digging. Fisher was trained as an architect at the University of Pennsylvania and dug at Nippur (1888–1890). He was involved in almost every American dig between the wars and, from 1925 until his death, was professor of archaeology at the American School in Jerusalem. The second step was developed by two British archaeologists, Kathleen Kenyon and Mortimer Wheeler, in respect to the Jericho dig and reported upon in 1952. The Wheeler-Kenyon method ran a deep trench and emphasized stratigraphic control. G. Ernest Wright, trained under William F. Albright, soon carried this method further at Shechem through systematic examination of potsherds. The final step was actually Sir William Matthew Flinders Petrie's simultaneous application of typology and stratigraphy at Tell el-Hesi in 1890, as will be pointed out below.

ects. So it was that Montgomery never taught me the magic bowl texts. Still, his study of them, *Aramaic Incantation Bowls from Nippur* (1913), remains a classic work, and anyone who wants to study the incantations should (and indeed must) read and digest Montgomery's book.

Instead of teaching me the magic bowl texts, Montgomery merely introduced me to the University of Pennsylvania Museum staff and requested that they grant me access to the collection. He showed me some large fragments that he had not included in his book and suggested that I publish them (which I eventually did). Montgomery also told me that the Sultan had kept part of the bowl collection for his museum in Istanbul and suggested that I ask Aziz Bey, director of the Museum of Antiquities in Istanbul, for permission to study and publish them. Montgomery assumed, incorrectly, that the Sultan had retained the cream of the collection for his own museum.

My voyage to the Near East in May–June 1931 took place before the era of regular air service across the Atlantic. In New York I boarded the *Patria,* a ship of the Messagerie Maritime Line, whose home port was Marseilles. The first stop was Boston; the next was Ponta Delgada in the Azores. The misty island rose like a fairyland out of the sea. On its steep sides peasants went about their chores with their donkeys. From there we sailed to Lisbon, where we anchored long enough to see some of the natural and cultural sights of that attractive city: my first contact with Europe.

From there we sailed south to the Straits of Gibraltar between North Africa and Spain and through the Straits into the Mediterranean, where our first stop was Marseilles. That port, the second largest city of France, meant more to me than to my fellow passengers. The Phoenicians have left an indelible mark there, including the long Phoenician inscription known as the Tariff of Marseilles. My background was beginning to give me the eyes to see the Mediterranean as a unit: the home of one great composite culture in any given era.

After Marseilles came stops at the Italian harbors of Genoa and Naples, and from there we headed south past the smoking island-volcano of Stromboli and through the Straits of Messina with lofty, erupting Mount Aetna on our starboard side. We skirted the north shore of Crete, where we were welcomed with festive lanterns and the Greek statesman Eleutherios Venizelos disembarked to visit his native island. We then sailed north to moor at Piraeus, the port of Athens.

Italy and Greece are both Mediterranean lands, but while Italy has the stronger European ties, Greece is more akin to the Near East. The Greeks recognize this in their language, for they call Greece *Hellas.* It is only when they have traveled out of Greece to Austria, Switzerland, or Italy that they refer to the terrain as *Avrupa* (= Europe). The difference between Greece and Italy is noticeable in the music, the food, and the character of the people.

Our two-day stopover in Athens gave me a chance to see the Acropolis with its incomparable Parthenon. In 1931, the pollution from auto exhaust had not yet damaged the stone of the Parthenon, as it has since then; nor had the wear and tear of tourism wrought its full measure of mischief. In 1931 the public could walk freely through the Parthenon; now the area is out of bounds.

Upon leaving Athens, the *Patria* crossed the Aegean and sailed up through the Dardanelles and across the Sea of Marmara to Istanbul. At that time, before the practice of erecting modern high-rise buildings, Istanbul and its stately minarets presented a wondrous sight. The travel schedule did not permit me to study the magic text bowls at that time, but I would return to complete that task not too far in the future (see below).

After leaving Istanbul, we returned to the Aegean and headed for Beirut, which was then an earthly paradise. Its beaches were a winter resort, while a mere hour away one encountered hills and mountains full of ideal summer resorts, where the peaks of Lebanon culminated in heights with eternal snows. Sadly, all this heaven-on-earth became an inferno because of prolonged ethnic violence less than half a century later.

My last stop on the *Patria* was the port of Jaffa. In 1931, passengers arriving at Jaffa on large vessels had to disembark with their baggage onto rowboats, which transported them between two large rocks and thence to shore. If the seas were rough, no one would attempt to row between the rocks; the ships would have to remain at anchor with all the passengers aboard until the storm subsided.

Jews landing in Jaffa typically fit into one of two categories: the younger ones coming in to build up the land, and the elderly who came to die and be buried in the holy soil of Palestine. The entire country was called Palestine at that time; the designation *Israel* was not applied to the region until the Jewish state was founded in 1948. *Palestine* did not become a politically loaded term until 1948. In fact, the leading English-language newspaper of the land was originally called *The Palestine Post*. It was only after 1948 that the paper adopted its present name, *The Jerusalem Post*.

After landing in Jaffa, I needed to hire a taxi to take me to Jerusalem, so I asked assistance from an Arab boatman in classical Arabic, which he did not understand. So I tried Hebrew and then English, neither of which he understood. Finally, the boatman inquired, "Efshar redst du zhargon" ("Perhaps you speak Yiddish"). I did and thus got the directions I needed.

The car took me to the American School of Oriental Research, where I met Professor William F. Albright,[10] who directed the school, especially

---

[10] William Foxwell Albright (1891–1971) took a doctorate at the Johns Hopkins University in 1916 under Paul Haupt. He was in Jerusalem at the ASOR School from 1918 until 1929, serving as director from 1921 to 1929. Because of his long stay in

during the summer seasons. In a few days I joined the expedition excavating the Maccabean Fortress of Beth-Sur,[11] west of the Arab town of Halhul in the region of Hebron. During this time, I was initiated into the archaeological techniques used by the American School.

The expedition was directed by Ovid Sellers,[12] a professor of Old Testament at McCormick Theological Seminary in Chicago. Sellers was a delightful companion. He composed humorous songs, which he sang as he accompanied himself on the guitar. A Christian scholar and a gentleman of exemplary life, he had the saving grace of ribaldry. When he and I in later years would meet at the often tedious annual meetings of the Society of Biblical Literature, he would greet me with the question, "Have you heard any good parables lately?"

Officially, Albright was only the technical archaeological advisor, but in reality he directed the expedition and made all the decisions on where and how to dig. He also trained the younger members of the staff, especially in ceramic typology and chronology. However, Sellers was responsible for composing the first edition of the excellent monograph that offered the final report on the excavation (1933).

Visiting the expedition was Clarence Fisher, a master field archaeologist with extensive experience excavating Mesopotamian, Egyptian, and Palestinian sites. Fisher also knew more than anyone else about the ceramics of ancient Palestine. Unfortunately, Fisher was plagued by troubles that sapped his strength and kept him from finishing his projects and thus from winning the fame that his mastery merited. Specifically, Fisher adopted a series of Arab boys who abandoned him after getting as much of his money as they could. Nevertheless, Fisher did supply Albright with the knowledge and the masterful drawings to proceed with ceramic chronology and typology. Thus, with Fisher's assistance, Albright completed his projects (especially his analysis of the pottery from Tell Beit Mirsim) and received the acclaim that follows from detailed, definitive publications. For my part, I will always remain indebted to Fisher, who took the trouble to explain to me at Beth-Sur the basic principles of "dirt" archaeology.

Palestine, his excavations, his publishing of detailed archaeology reports and the larger history of the Middle and Near East, and his training of many archaeologists and Old and New Testament scholars at Johns Hopkins, Albright was one of the most influential archaeologists of his era.

[11] The excavation began in 1931 under the auspices of McCormick Theological Seminary in Chicago. In 1957 Ovid R. Sellers returned to conduct a second campaign.

[12] Sellers (1884–1975) studied at the University of Chicago and McCormick Theological Seminary before taking his Ph.D. at Johns Hopkins. He was Professor of Old Testament Language and Literature at McCormick for over thirty years. During 1948–1949 he was director of the ASOR Jerusalem School.

While at Beth-Sur, I also saw firsthand the dangers of library research without field experience. The Maccabeans had prepared cisterns in the bedrock to catch water during the winter rains. When we showed one armchair archaeologist the Maccabean cisterns (which just happened to be full of water and mud from the rains of the previous winter), he exclaimed in wonder: "Just think of it! From the Maccabean period, and still wet!" Although this man was an expert on Palestinian geography and topography at Hebrew University in Jerusalem, he lacked the field experience that can help one avoid such a *faux pas*.

In those days I liked to wrestle to keep fit. So after work on the dig ended at sunset, I used to wrestle with a young, husky staff member from Iowa, H. Milton Patterson. The local sheikh, a man named Yusuf, often came to watch us. In those days, the nonurban Arabs did not indulge in contact sports. In addition, men of standing in the rural communities dressed modestly in long robes that covered them from the head down to the wrists and ankles. In short, they never exposed any part of the body other than face, hands and feet. Once, while watching one of our wrestling matches, Albright asked Sheikh Yusuf, "So what do you think of the American sport of wrestling?" The dignified Arab chief replied, "Knowledge of it must come from Allah, and whatever comes from Allah is good. But would it not be more efficacious if they used daggers?"

Between 1931 and 1935, I was able to visit the American School of Oriental Research in Jerusalem on numerous occasions. There I was privileged to meet a number of distinguished archaeologists, including Sir William Matthew Flinders Petrie, the foremost creator of modern archaeology.[13] Petrie had developed the principle of stylistic development of artifacts so that one could assign sequence dates to the various stages. He had accomplished this by arranging Egyptian pots with wavy-ledge handles in sequence of their development, then establishing a "sequence date" for each stage. Some time later Wilhelm Dörpfeld (1853–1940), the architect of the Heinrich Schliemann (1822–1890) excavations at Troy, showed that the successive strata forming a mound yield a series of relative dates, for each stratum is later than the one beneath it. When Petrie excavated Tell el-Hesi in 1890 and applied simultaneously the principles of stratification (i.e., the chronological sequence of strata) and typology (i.e., the sequence dates of artifacts, especially of the ubiquitous pottery), modern scientific archaeology was born.

---

[13] Flinders Petrie (1853–1942) was born in England and did not receive formal education, although he apprenticed as a surveyor. Through his explorations in Egypt and Palestine, he became conversant with Egyptology and with Egyptian and Palestinian archaeology. He became connected with the University of London in 1892. He completed a survey of the pyramids and fifty Egyptian cities in 1929, publishing over a hundred volumes pertaining to Egypt.

Petrie was not an academician, but a genius with keen powers of observation who went wherever the facts might lead him. He generally held a low opinion of other archaeologists. When I visited his dig in the Philistine plain at Tell el-ʿAjjul, I congratulated him for finding more gold jewelry there than all the archaeologists had unearthed in the preceding century at all the Palestinian sites combined. He replied that his dull-witted rivals were wasting their efforts at the towns where Israelite prophets had bequeathed the books that bear their names in the Bible. He explained that spirituality does not produce golden treasures; he merely used common sense to excavate a city of the "sinful" Philistines, who were known to have carried on the artistic traditions of the high culture of Crete and the Aegean.

On the day of my visit to Petrie, excitement filled the air. Armed police stood guard as heavy crates were hoisted onto a postal department truck. A crowd of local Arabs watched the entire process until the loaded truck drove off, bound for Jerusalem. Petrie then took me into the tent that served as his office and explained that, although it appeared that his golden treasures had been shipped to Jerusalem for safekeeping, the crates contained only sand. Petrie then informed me that he had, in fact, buried the treasures under various beds and furnishings. There they would rest securely without attracting the notice of robbers.

Petrie also showed me the photographic equipment housed in his work-tent. He had pioneered the use of time-exposed photographs of artifacts to illustrate the annual reports of his excavations, but not because he alone had access to the latest or finest equipment. In fact, his camera obscura was a ladies' hatbox; the tiny aperture was made with a hat pin. The wooden tripod that held the camera was so warped that it was wobbly. When I informed him that a steel warp-proof tripod could be purchased in Jerusalem, he replied that his wooden tripod was the original, whereas all others were merely imitations that he would not think of using. One might say that Petrie was excessively appreciative of his own epoch-making originality.

Petrie's wife, Lady Hilda, had been a beauty in her youth, and she was still quite attractive on the threshold of old age. She idolized her husband and shared his commitment to archaeological work. Once, for example, a staff member asked if she might have a little hot water with which to wash before breakfast. Sir Flinders flatly refused and noted that he and Lady Hilda washed before going to bed so that there would be no need to waste precious water in the morning. On waking up, it sufficed Sir Flinders and Lady Hilda to rub their hands with a little sand. The British archaeologists in those days made a fetish of living a rugged life in the field.

My old friend Samuel Yeivin, who became the first Director of Antiquities of the State of Israel in 1948, gave me further insight into Petrie. Earlier in his career, Yeivin had served as an archaeological assistant to

Petrie in Egypt and had drawn the plan of a temple they had unearthed. The following year they discovered an additional wing of the temple, so Yeivin asked Petrie for the plan so he could add the new discovery to it. "Unfortunately," Petrie replied, "I buried the plan you gave me last year, but I do not remember exactly where. As soon as I recall the place, I'll retrieve the plan and give it to you so that you can make the addition." That was nearly a century ago. Both Petrie and Yeivin have died, and the buried plan has not yet been recovered.

Petrie possessed a phenomenal memory and scorned reliance on notes. He was successively forbidden to excavate in Egypt and Palestine because of such deviations from standard procedures. The lesson to be learned from this comedy of errors is that the best of memories can and will fail. Furthermore, all memories are terminated by death. Standard operating procedure requires the maintenance of written records in all scientific fields, including archaeology. Exceptions should not be made, not even for geniuses.

Among Petrie's numerous virtues was his habit of sending to press a volume reporting the work and results of his expedition every year. Many archaeologists take years, even decades, to publish their final reports. Even worse, all too many final reports never appear. The discoveries that have been unearthed are in effect reburied and sometimes lost forever. Such was not the case with Petrie. His yearly reports, plus many other books on Egyptology and other special themes, fill shelves upon shelves. Once, at a tea reception in Jerusalem, a well-meaning lady said to Petrie, "Oh, Sir Flinders, I am so happy to meet you. I have read all of your books." Petrie, prolific author that he was, responded, "Madame, no one has read all of my books."

I would like to tell much more about Petrie, but in this autobiographical sketch I will limit myself to only one more illustration. At Megiddo, the excavators, who had discovered what they thought were the stables of Solomon, sought Petrie's advice on where to look for the governor's palace. Petrie walked around and spit into the air a number of times to determine the direction of the prevailing winds. He then advised the Chicago excavators to dig upwind because they could be sure that the governor would avoid the smells of the stables. In relating this anecdote of the great Petrie, I am not inferring that his every step or premise turned out to be correct. I merely want to describe the originality of a genius at work.

I was fortunate that Petrie took a liking to me. I think he did so partly because I was so young that there was reason to hope that I might not become a member of the Establishment that he scorned so much. I like to believe that such hopes were not entirely unjustified.

A second scholar I had the good fortune to meet at this time was Père Marie-Joseph Lagrange (1855–1938) of the Dominican École Biblique. I went to the École often because it possessed the best library in Jerusalem. I admired Lagrange for a variety of reasons, not least of which was his commitment to scholarship. Against heavy odds, Lagrange had waged and finally won the long battle that breached the wall between Catholic scholarship and international biblical criticism.[14] Lagrange's first love was the Old Testament, but he was forbidden by the Holy See to pursue this area of study because, at the turn of the century (ca. 1900), higher criticism of the Old Testament was the focal point of controversy. Thus, Lagrange turned to the New Testament and wrote commentaries on all four Gospels.

When I appeared on the scene in Jerusalem from 1931 to 1935, Père Lagrange's victory was manifested in programs of the highest level of scholarship at the Jesuit Pontificium Institutum Biblicum in Rome and at the Dominican École Biblique in Jerusalem. It is not generally recognized that such "liberalism" in the Church did not start with the physical or social sciences but with the highly sensitive area of biblical scholarship.

While at Jerusalem I also spent time with Hayyim Nahman Bialik (1873–1934). I first met Bialik about 1925 when he lectured at the University of Pennsylvania. His mouth was full of gold teeth, and he looked nothing like a poet, though he was without question a great one. In 1931 I was privileged to be invited to his home on Bialik Street in Tel Aviv for Shabbat.

I admired Bialik, but I was troubled by rumors that he was buying up orange groves near Jaffa, hardly a fitting activity for the greatest Hebrew poet since Old Testament times. Some years later, however, I came to understand why Bialik did what he did. I asked an authority on Bialik's life and works why he wasted his time making money that he did not need. I received a clear answer. Bialik had suffered so much from poverty and hunger in Europe that he could not rid himself of the fear of lapsing into them again. I was also in Jerusalem when Bialik died on July 4, 1934. I will never forget the outpouring of grief by the Jewish men, women, and children that attended that sad day.

After the 1931 summer campaign at Beth-Sur ended in August, I traveled by ship back to Istanbul. There, following the advice of my mentor Montgomery, I would study the Aramaic magic bowls housed at the Museum of Antiquities. The collection of bowls was not as large as I (or Montgomery) had expected, so I had plenty of time during the month of September to make facsimiles of the bowls and to take the necessary notes for publication, as well as plenty of leisure time to see the glories of Istanbul. During my lunch hours at the Museum of Antiquities, I frequently took time to admire the magnificent sarcophagus that is popularly (but incorrectly) known as "the sarcophagus of Alexander." I also viewed the imperial splendors in the Topkapi and the beautiful mosques.

Little did I suspect that these incantation bowls from Babylonian sites would establish a thread that has woven its way throughout my studies and teaching during my entire career. I have since published the texts of Aramaic

---

[14] Lagrange also founded the esteemed journal, *Revue Biblique,* in 1892.

bowls from collections in the United States, Great Britain, France, Sweden, Turkey, Israel, Iraq, and Iran. The significance of these bowls in my professional career mirrors the importance of magic in human culture. For example, ancient Greece nurtured more magicians and their superstitious clients than philosophers and scientists, and more ancient Israelites resorted to magic than enriched the world with the Law, Prophets, and Psalms of David. Moreover, magic is quite syncretistic and an excellent channel for the diffusion of culture. Obviously, exorcisms are much easier to learn than Greek philosophy or the ins and outs of Hebrew social justice, which helps explain their broad appeal. Although the texts I have studied are mainly in "respectable" areas such as law, economics, and history, it has become evident to me that some study of magical texts can help us to avoid the common error of regarding humanity as a rational species.[15]

In addition to studying the Aramaic magic bowls and exploring the riches of the area, I also made many friends in Istanbul. I met, for example, Michael Avi-Yonah, a local Sephardic Jew who later migrated to Palestine and became Israel's leading authority on ancient Jewish art. I also encountered a Turkish law student named Nuri Bey, who showed me around and introduced me to a number of his friends. Nuri Bey was an ardent admirer of Mustafa Kemal Ataturk (then known as the Ghazi "Conqueror"), the great reformer who changed the Turkish script from the Arabic to the Latin alphabet in 1928. Mustafa Kemal also disestablished Islam and made Turkey into a secular state, emancipated women, and made numerous other radical but lasting changes.

My 1931 sojourn in Istanbul took place less than a decade after the Ghazi had abolished the Sultanate, the Caliphate, and polygamy. One day I asked Nuri Bey about a certain group of forlorn-looking men. Nuri explained that they were the eunuchs who had been important members of the imperial court but who were now the unemployed flotsam and jetsam of an abolished profession. Many years later I revisited Istanbul and saw Nuri Bey. He had changed his opinion of Mustafa Kemal drastically. Nuri now felt that Mustafa Kemal had committed an irreparable blunder, cutting off all of Ottoman literature from the rising generations, who can no longer even read the script of Turkish documents published before 1928.

Digging in Iraq

After a fruitful month in Istanbul, I traveled to Mosul to meet the expedition staff that was to be based in the nearby Yezidi village of Bahshika,

---

[15] See "The Aramaic Incantation Bowls in Historic Perspective," in *Minḥah le-Naḥum: Biblical and Other Studies Presented to Nahum M. Sarna in Honour of his 70th Birthday* (JSOTSup 154; ed. M. Brettler and M. Fishbane; Sheffield: Sheffield Academic Press, 1993), 142–46.

northeast of Mosul in Iraqian Kurdistan. I arrived a few days before my expedition colleagues, so I checked in at the best hotel in town (which was none too good according to Western standards) to wait for them. The hotel manager, wanting to take care of me, asked whether I wouldn't prefer to have my meals served in my room rather than in the dining hall, where guests were regaled with floor-show entertainment. Like any normal twenty-three-year-old, I chose the latter. But later that evening I understood why the manager suggested that I dine alone in my room.

The hotel restaurant was the favorite cabaret of Kurdish tribesmen who lived in the region. I had a table to myself, but quite close by was a table at which two Kurds were drinking ʿaraq. All at once, one of them pulled his dagger out of its scabbard and began to wave it near his companion's neck. This alarmed me so that I told the waiter to fetch the manager, who promptly came. I informed the manager about the knife-play at the adjacent table, but it did not disturb him in the least. He explained that in Kurdistan this was all done in fun, that "they only flash their daggers but do not stab each other." I thanked him for his comforting words, yet I could not enjoy eating my meal or watching the belly dancers while these inebriated Kurds continued their knife-play. My misgivings proved to be justified, for two nights later there was a fatal stabbing in the hotel cabaret.

One might fault the manager's "boys will be boys in Kurdistan" attitude, but if he had not allowed armed men to drink in the cabaret, he would have been inviting bankruptcy. In those days, the stray bullet was said to be the most frequent cause of death in Kurdistan. Shooting (if only up into the air) was a normal expression of exuberance and joy in Iraq, especially among trigger-happy Kurdish mountaineers.

After my colleagues arrived, we left for the village of Bahshika, where we had rented a house in which to live and to establish our expedition headquarters. The residents of Bahshika and the nearby village of Bahzani are Arabic speaking, but they can also communicate in Kurdish. The latter is important for them because they are not Muslims but Yezidis, who elsewhere speak Kurdish as their primary, and often only, language.

The Yezidis (whom outsiders incorrectly call "Devil Worshipers") adhere to a dualistic religion. They believe that God is exclusively good and incapable of doing anything evil or harmful. Thus, although one can love God, it is useless to pray to him because he cannot and will not harm anyone. Satan, however, is the Prince of Evil and must be propitiated so that he will refrain from harming a person. The Yezidis in those days believed that he so abhors the pejorative name *Satan* that they refrained from pronouncing not only it but also any word that resembled it phonetically. Consequently, when members of the expedition staff conversed in English, they had to avoid saying "shut the door" because the consonants of *shut* are the same as the first two consonants of *Shaytan* (Satan). In order not to terrify any of our Yezidi servants, we would say, "close the door." The Yezidis, for their part, referred to the Prince of Evil by honorific titles such "The Peacock Angel." In fact, a bronze peacock represents him iconographically at the central mountain shrine at Sheikh Adi in the Jebel Sinjar.

Ordinarily groups of Muslims worked harmoniously on our excavations in the same areas as groups of Yezidis. However, during the month of Ramadan we had to keep them far apart. During Ramadan, the Muslims, who worked all day long without eating, drinking, or smoking, became dangerously intolerant toward the "idolatrous" Yezidis. Ethnic fasting is not conducive to neighborliness.

Ephraim Speiser had been excavating two mounds near Bahshika under the auspices of ASOR. Our expedition continued this work, excavating both mounds simultaneously. One, called Tell Billa, contained interesting Hurrian remains and was located quite near to Bahshika. We believed that this mound was known as Shibaniba in antiquity, for the city gate at Nineveh that led toward Tell Billa was named The Shibaniba Gate. During the first year I was on the dig, we unearthed tablets on Tell Billa that referred to Shibaniba by name, which confirmed our identification.

The other mound we were excavating was Tepe Gawra, which means "high mound." It was a fitting name, for the mound was just that. The steep site had been formed by over twenty successive settlements coming almost to a point at the topmost level, which consisted of the ruins of a single fortress constructed about 1500 B.C.E. There was no room for any later settlement. This site proved to be of great value for the study of stratified occupation going back deep into early Neolithic times. The Neolithic ceramics there were often of such high quality that they made archaeological history.

I more or less alternated days supervising the actual excavating on Billa and Gawra. The latter gave me precious experience in the materials of prehistory, but I had already determined to concentrate on the literate ages, after ca. 3000 B.C.E., when Sumerian texts first appear. Prior to the age of archaeological discoveries, the study of history began with the Bible and classical texts (ca. 1500 B.C.E.) When Sumerian was added, archaeology threw the beginning back to 3000 B.C.E. All of our knowledge of the history before the age of writing comes from archaeology, that is, from artifacts and ancient stratified towns and cities.

One day during my first year in Iraqian field work (1931–1932), I was driving from Bahshika to Tepe Gawra. It was necessary to cross a narrow wadi along the way, a wadi that was dry except after a downpour of rain. That day I nearly struck a boulder that had been placed at the bottom of the wadi. After work, I invited the chief of police in Bahshika to have tea with me so I could tell him about the boulder. He assured me that he would take care of matters so that it would never happen again.

So, the following Sunday he and I drove to a nearby village (chosen at random), where he told me to drive up to the mayor's house and toot the horn. When the mayor came out, the police chief ordered him, "Come back with us to the police station in Bahshika, where we will beat you for putting the boulder in the wadi." The mayor protested, "By my head and by my eyes, I did not do it—but I know who did: three shepherds from another village." He then gave us the names of the shepherds and told us in which village they lived. So we drove there and ordered the mayor of that village to turn the shepherds over to us. All of them denied any guilt, but they were flogged the following morning in Bahshika anyway. When I asked the police chief whether he was sure that they were the actual culprits, he replied, "Of course not. In America, you punish the criminals. In Iraq, we punish the crime. Iraq is a very gossipy land. Everybody knows what's going on in the neighborhood, and you can be sure that the people whom we have beaten will make life miserable for the real culprits. In any case, the offense will not recur." Nor did it during the rest of our time there, which ended in 1935.

Ephraim A. Speiser directed the excavations at Billa and Gawra my first year in the field (1931–1932).[16] Charles Bache, who was quite different from Speiser and who had no formal training in ancient Near Eastern studies, assumed the position of director the following years. Bache was a "practical" man who had drifted from one thing to another until he somehow wound up in field archaeology, where he tried to become a systematic excavator. Bache's connections with Horace Jayne, Director of the University of Pennsylvania Museum, played a significant role in his appointment, but Speiser also favored Bache because he wanted a weak substitute in the field, one who would not threaten his "remote control" of what went on at the dig.

We saw a great deal of the University of Chicago staff excavating at Khorsabad, a rich Assyrian site near Tepe Gawra. At that time, many field archaeologists engaged in heavy drinking, which took a toll in deaths, especially but far from exclusively on a number of Chicago expeditions. I did not feel much professional kinship with my colleagues or with our Khorsabad neighbors because, I felt, they lacked dedication to the work.

---

[16] Speiser (1902–1965) was born in the Galician region of Poland and began his studies in Austria. He migrated to the United States at age eighteen. He took an M.A. from the University of Pennsylvania in 1923, working under Montgomery and with Margolis at Dropsie. The next year he wrote his dissertation under Margolis at Dropsie. In 1931 he became a full professor at the University of Pennsylvania and concurrently at Dropsie. Early in his career, Speiser worked in Near East and Middle Eastern languages, especially the Akkadian dialect of Nuzi and in Hurrian. In his later years he focused upon the Old Testament.

Gordon Loud, director of the Khorsabad excavations, eventually left archaeology completely. Our assistant director (Paul Beidler), a talented architect whom I liked as a companion, had only wanted to achieve the position of assistant director and then abandon archaeology as his profession forever, which is exactly what he did after the 1932–1933 campaign. I do not sit in judgment of people who use work opportunities as steppingstones. I simply feel little or no kinship with anyone who lacks a "calling."

In February 1932 I completed a short tour of duty at Ur in Sumer to serve as the epigrapher for the director, Major (later Sir) C. Leonard Woolley.[17] The site still abounded in unexcavated Royal Tombs of Ur, which yielded new treasures of gold, silver, carnelian, and lapis lazuli.

Woolley was a superb field archaeologist with a knack for "proving the Bible" to the satisfaction of well-heeled and God-fearing widows. For example, when he found a sculpture of a buck grazing on a tree, he identified it with "the ram caught in a thicket" (Gen 22:13). The widows, and the general public, gladly overlooked the irreconcilable discrepancies. But the most serious blunder that he succeeded in canonizing for the Establishment was identifying Sumerian Ur as the birthplace of Abraham. Granted, the origins of this error predated him. No author before the mid-nineteenth century had ever located Ur of the Chaldees in the south. But with the decipherment of cuneiform about the middle of the nineteenth century, the name of Ur in Sumer emerged, at which point some proposed the interesting (but untenable) identification of this site with Abraham's Ur of the Chaldees. To be sure, the dazzling treasures that Woolley discovered at Ur, rendered the place "worthy of Father Abraham."

Woolley had married late in life. His wife was a beautiful but somewhat difficult young woman who treated staff members rather high-handedly. For example, she had a living room with a fireplace, but the staff was typically not invited to visit it. She also had a pet dog that needed discipline from time to time. Because she did not want her pet to hold anything against her, she would make a young American on the staff (I believe his name was Richardson) spank the naughty dog.

During my somewhat brief time at Ur, she invited me to see her sumptuous living room. I suspect that she hoped that, when I returned to Bahshika, I would spread news of its splendor among my American colleagues. But I had taken a dislike to her and repeatedly declined her invitations. (In my youth, I was quite undiplomatic.) Not to be thwarted, she

---

[17] Sir C. Leonard Woolley (1880–1960) was born in London. He attended New College, Oxford, and became there an assistant in the Ashmolean Museum. He was involved in a 1912 expedition to Carchemish, sponsored by the British Museum. In 1922 he was involved in excavations at Ur in Sumer. During 1946–1949 he dug at Tell Atchana north of Antioch in Turkey.

complained to her husband, who called me aside and asked me to accept her next invitation. I did, and thus peace was restored between us. Although I have characterized Lady Woolley as difficult, I have come to realize that, in different ways, I too used to be difficult. Yet I think (and trust) that I have mellowed with the years.

Lady Woolley performed at least one good deed at the Ur expedition house, namely, she introduced Max Mallowan to Agatha Christie there. In time the romance that started at Ur resulted in the felicitous marriage of Lady (and eventually Dame) Agatha to Sir Max. Agatha was witty, which served her well in the union. Agatha happened to be considerably older than Max, but this did not bother her at all, for, as she said, "It is wonderful to be the wife of an archaeologist because the older you are, the more interested he is in you."

My visit to Ur was memorable in many ways. Though not a humanistic scholar, Woolley was a master archaeologist and an outstanding discoverer. I feel lucky to have known him and to have served as his epigrapher early in 1932. In addition, I had the good fortune to share a train compartment with André Parrot, who was en route to the French excavations at Lagash while I was traveling to Ur.[18] Parrot would later direct the epoch-making excavations at Mari and become the curator of the Mesopotamian section of the Louvre. When we met on the train, he could not speak English, nor was I able to converse in French. Fortunately, both of us could converse in colloquial Iraqian Arabic. Both of us had become fluent in this language through our dealings with the Iraqi laborers who did the actual digging for our respective expeditions. Moreover, since he and I were both engaged in Iraqian excavations, our vocabulary was adequate, even for discussing the technical details of our work.

Upon returning to Bahshika, I resumed work on both mounds, on the days it did not rain. Heavy winter rains often kept our staff house-bound, with time for most staff members to play cards and drink, neither of which appealed to me. I preferred to spend my spare time, in the evenings and on rainy days, reading the recently published autographed copies of the Nuzi tablets.

Each Sunday we would suspend excavations and take the day off. If the weather permitted, we could walk to interesting spots in the vicinity. One Sunday as Khidr, the architect's assistant, and I were walking, we

---

[18] André Parrot (1901–1980) was born in Desandans, France. He studied at the French School of Archaeology in Jerusalem. From 1931 to 1967 he was involved in digs at tells in Iraq. He dug at Mari between 1933 and 1974, where more than twenty thousand tablets were found from the royal palace archives. In 1936 he was appointed to the Protestant faculty of the University of Paris and in 1937 became a professor at the École du Louvre.

passed a spring emerging from a mountain cavern. This prompted me to ask why the Yezidis built a shrine at every spring. Looking at me with amazement, he replied, "How can we not adore God, wherever he miraculously brings forth water from stone?" It was then that I realized that pre-scientific natives see the poetic miracle of nature. We Westerners, however, regard nature as a kind of plumbing system operated by physical forces such as pressure and gravity. Nothing is more prosaic than plumbing.

Springtime in Paris, Learning French

Because I had taught myself French, I could understand written French with ease, but I could not converse in French. To rectify this situation, I decided to spend two months of free time, from mid-April to mid-June 1932, living with a French family in Paris. With the help of a newspaper advertisement, I found an interesting family who took in paying guests who would live in their apartment and take meals at their French-speaking table. The house was located near the Bois de Boulogne.

The head of this household was one Mme. la Baronne de Duclas, whose two children lived with her: a teenage son and a twelve-year-old daughter. I needed colloquial experience in French at a very simple level, so I decided to spend time talking with the youngest family member. Thus, during my first week to ten days in Paris, I often took the twelve-year-old daughter out boating on a lake in the Bois de Boulogne. As we rowed we talked about simple matters that would interest a twelve-year-old, and soon I was prepared to plunge into conversations with adults.

The social circle of the baroness included the ousted nobility and ex-royalty of Europe. Interestingly enough, they regarded the Napoleonic pretenders, not the commoners or antimonarchists, as their foes in France. Among the many fine people who graced Sunday meetings at the baroness's apartment, the most elegant and distinguished were the Russian Prince Galicin (also spelled Golitsyn) and his beautiful wife. During the week he drove a taxi, but on Sundays he looked and dressed like the aristocrat that he was. The communist revolution in Russia obliged many gentlemen to drive taxis in Paris and many noble ladies to live as long as they could by selling off their jewels. A worse fate had befallen those who remained in the Soviet Union.

The social circle of La Baronne de Duclas seemed to me a fairyland, where the French royalists expected the restoration of the Bourbon kings, and the Russians the restoration of the Romanov Tsars. Their blind faith reminded me of religious fanatics who await the imminent coming of the Messiah. People frequently do not believe in the probable, but rather in what they want to believe.

My stay in Paris was of interest in many ways. I spent much time in the Louvre, where I copied magic bowls for publication. I also worked on my first book in Paris, a monograph on *Nouns in the Nuzu Tablets,* which was published in Paris in 1936. I also audited lectures by French savants such as Charles Virolleaud, little knowing that my primary work in life (Ugaritic) would be based on his pioneering contributions and that eventually we would become close friends.[19]

During my stay I also met other prominent experts on the ancient Near East: René Dussaud, Georges Contenau, and the great cuneiformist François Thureau-Dangin. The best measure of the latter's genius is his translation of the old royal Sumerian inscriptions, which he first published in 1907. Subsequent translators who deviated from him in their zeal to be original usually produced inferior work. Sumerian, which is unrelated to other Near Eastern languages, is important because it is the earliest known language with a written literature anywhere in the world. As such, it exercised a great influence on all subsequent civilization. Our understanding of Sumerian grammar and lexicography is now highly refined, thanks largely to Thureau-Dangin's accurate translations and meticulous analysis of the script and language.

In 1936 I called on Thureau-Dangin in his office at the Louvre. He was not only a scholar but an aristocrat who owned large estates with hunting lodges. In fact, he had just returned from hunting, on horseback, wild boars on his land. But he was, at this time, quite deaf. In the days before modern hearing aids, the best the deaf could do was to place a large horn to an ear. Thus, although I could understand his French with ease, he had a difficult time understanding my French pronunciation shouted into his horn. Fortunately, the Assyriologist Julius Lewy had advised me to address questions or to make comments to Thureau-Dangin in English on slips of paper, and this mode of conversation worked beautifully.

I had, by the time of our discussion in 1936, published articles on cuneiform tablets, Aramaic incantations, and other topics. Indeed, Thureau-Dangin had cited some of my writings, always favorably. Among his compliments to me that day was a remark that I was destined to contribute to the bright future of cuneiform studies. Exactly what Thureau-Dangin had in mind, I will never know. But I do know that these encouraging words addressed to me, barely twenty-eight years old, by the greatest Assyriologist of all time inspired me to persevere in the decades ahead when the going was rough.

Return to Palestine

During the winter of 1932–1933, I was to serve on the field staff at the Judean site of Tell Beit Mirsim, under the direction of William F. Albright,

---

[19] Charles Virolleaud (1879–1986) became famous as a French epigrapher of cuneiform. He held posts at the École des Langues Orientales of the Sorbonne and at the University of Lyons (1905–1912). He worked on the tablets from Ras Shamra, taking the lead in making them available to scholars, and in 1930 determined the complete Ugaritic alphabet.

who was then at the height of his intellectual powers. Albright focused his main attention on the ceramics there, and his publication of the Tell Beit Mirsim pottery was a landmark in the typology and the chronology of Palestinian ceramics. Every working day he spent considerable time examining sherds unearthed in each excavated room and training his young assistants to master Palestinian ceramics. Among us disciples, G. Ernest Wright and especially Nelson Glueck deserve mention.[20]

In addition to the hours I spent daily on the mound, I spent a great deal of time in the headquarters tent drawing restored pots and characteristic fragments. I had already decided that written records would be the main focus of my scholarship, but I recognized that artifacts (especially ceramics) were important, and I wanted to have adequate knowledge of all the evidence for reconstructing the human past. It is important to know how much is enough of each contributing discipline.

Our laborers on this expedition came from the village of Dhahariyya. In the summer they lived in the cool caves of the area, but winters in their houses could be quite uncomfortable. One of the workmen, named Isa, was quite strong, so we employed him to break heavy boulders with a sledgehammer so the pieces could be carried off to the dump. One day Isa told me how he avoided the discomforts of the cold season. At the onset of winter, he would steal a camel as amateurishly as possible so as to ensure getting caught. As punishment, the British authorities would put him in jail for the entire winter.

He further explained that in the old days the Ottoman prisons were dirty and cold and that, unless one's family brought goodies from the outside, the food was inadequate and scarcely edible. But the British jails were comfortable. The fare was good and actually included meat at least once

---

[20] G. Ernest Wright (1909–1974) studied with Ovid Sellers at McCormick Theological Seminary and took his doctorate under William F. Albright at Johns Hopkins University. He began his field experience in Palestine under Albright and became especially adept at classifying and dating pottery. He later undertook major digs at Bethel, Shechem, and Gezer. Wright taught at McCormick Theological Seminary (1938–1958), then at Harvard Divinity School until his death.

Nelson Glueck (1900–1971) was born in Cincinnati, Ohio, of Lithuanian immigrants and received his Ph.D. from the University of Jena in 1925. He came under the influence of Albright in the late 1920s at Tell Beit Mirsim. He was noted for his monumental explorations of the Transjordan, the Negev, and other regions. He also excavated at a Nabatean temple in Khirbet et Tannur; Tell el Kheleifeh, which he thought was Ezion-geber, Solomon's seaport; and in later years at Gezer. He served several stints as director of the ASOR Jerusalem School between 1932 and 1947. In 1948 he became president of Hebrew Union College and in 1963 established the Hebrew Union College Biblical and Archaeological School in Jerusalem.

a week. Moreover, the police saw to it that prisoners got a reasonable amount of exercise and periodical changes of clean clothes. Isa had nothing but praise for the British Empire, whose blessings he especially enjoyed every winter.

The Arab villages all had a generous share of distinctive personalities. Even the demimonde in America is devoid of an Isa's charm. I have never encountered an American auto thief who hopes to get caught in order to enjoy being a seasonal guest of a much-loved government. Of course, times have changed. The adjective *evil* is now automatically applied to the noun *empire*. We want the entire world to have independence, freedom, and American-style democracy, for which most of the world is still unprepared. As I follow developments in the Near East, I wistfully recall those relatively good old days when the British and French mandates kept the lid on and empires were not ipso facto evil.

At the close of the summer campaign at Tell Beit Mirsim, I had over a month to spend in Palestine before the start of the winter campaign in Iraq. So I decided to reside at the home of Dr. Yitshaq Epstein, which Mrs. Epstein ran as a pension. The primary benefit of the pension was the opportunity to converse in Hebrew at mealtimes. In those days the best Hebrew was spoken by Yitshaq Epstein and David Yellin, both highly respected holders of Ph.D.'s in linguistics. They exerted considerable influence on the development of Hebrew as a living language.

Epstein's Hebrew was elegantly European. Unless one was addressing a relative or close friend, one did not use the pronouns ʾ*atta* or ʾ*att* (the masc. sg. and fem. sg. forms for *you*) but rather *kevodo*, "his honor," or *kevodah*, "her honor." Such courtesy has disappeared in contemporary Hebrew, as has a phonetic accuracy and the richness of vocabulary and idiom derived from a knowledge of biblical, rabbinic, medieval, and early modern Hebrew literature. A pioneering nation, with immigrants from the ends of the earth and surrounded by enemies, cannot maintain the cultural and linguistic standards that Yitshaq Epstein and David Yellin fostered in the 1930s.

In order to understand the educated urban Arabs, I spent a good part of my months in Jerusalem living with the Wehbe family. I did this all four years that I spent as a fellow of the American Schools. The Wehbes were Christians who had left their native Arab church in order to join the Russian Orthodox Church. Unlike the Arab villagers I knew as laborers at Beth-Sur and Tell Beit Mirsim, the Wehbes were well educated in Arabic, English, and Hebrew. They had one son and three daughters. The latter, who ranged in age from about eighteen to twenty-five, lived at home with their parents and spoke Arabic with each other. Because I had been trained in classical written Arabic and had experience in the colloquial dialects, I had no difficulty conversing with them in Arabic. Granted, at first much of what

I said sounded quaint, but I gradually learned to speak what could be described as upper-class Jerusalem Arabic. The youngest daughter, who had the Russian name "Louba," often invited me to parties, where I met many Christian Arabs. This kind of social experience would not have been possible in traditional Muslim circles, in which men belonged to one society and women to another.

There was, in those days, some tension between Jews and non-Jews, but there was no barrier to warm friendship on an individual basis. I remember talking with an Arab from Hebron as we rode on a bus to Tel Aviv one Friday. He told me he was on his way to spend the Sabbath with his "best friend" in Tel Aviv. When I asked whether religion caused any problems, he replied, "None whatsoever! My friend is not interested in buying my land in Hebron, nor would I sell it to him or to anyone else. We are simply best friends, and his family expects me to stay with them every Sabbath." The problem in Palestine has not been between individuals, but between groups. Westerners often fail to reckon with the difference between mass psychology and personal relationships.

Tragic events in Iraq at the end of the 1932–1933 campaign made it unadvisable to return to Tell Billa and Tepe Gawra in 1933–1934. Thus, I was directed to spend that year at the Jerusalem School participating in its archaeological program. Not only did I look forward to spending a winter season in Palestine for the first time, I also welcomed the prospect of working with and learning from Albright, who was scheduled to be at that branch for part of that winter.

During the final months of 1933, Albright conducted an excavation at Ader in Transjordan, the region known as Moab in antiquity. Some of the workmen told me that at night lightning had often been seen issuing from a cave and that this could only mean that the kings of Moab were buried there. Such thinking makes no sense to Westerners, but to the local Arabs nothing could be clearer. I told Albright, who felt that it would do no harm to excavate into the cave, and he put me in charge of the operation.

In the morning, however, I was confronted with a serious labor problem: a strike. The spokesman of the striking Arabs explained, "We would face normal dangers for you, but we dare not rouse the ire of the kings of Moab buried in the cave." I decided at that moment that the only way to overcome this psychological barrier was to appeal to their sense of honor. To that end, I delivered an Arabic oration that went something as follows:

> I have come to you from across the seven seas, and I shall soon return to tell the world about the men of Ader. Do you want me to describe you as mice or lions? The mouse is a wretched creature who fears even the cat, while the lion roars and terrifies both man and beast. Shall I say you are mice or lions?

After a tense minute of silence, they began to shout, "We are lions!" Then I asked, "And do you know where the lion has his lair? In the cave! So take up your picks, O my lions, and hack away to clear the cave. Who are you, O men of Ader?" In a chorus they exclaimed, "We are your lions!" and dug into the cave furiously.

A few days later they had cleared the cave. We did not find the tomb of the kings of Moab. Still, I had founded the first "Lions Club" in Transjordan, and for this, Albright described me as a genius. Since that week in 1933 the Near East has become more sophisticated as well as more dangerous. Unfortunately, my *genius* in personnel management can no longer solve the problems of the region. Alas, for the now-lost innocence I found in the men of Ader nearly seventy years ago!

Albright had an apparent dread of women that I still find hard to understand. True, he respected women such as Dorothy Garrod, the first woman professor at Cambridge University, and praised her archaeological work in the Mount Carmel caves, with their remains of the Neanderthaloid Homo Palestinensis.[21] But he did not allow women on expedition staffs no matter how qualified and competent they were. On at least one occasion, however, Albright did not succeed in barring a woman from his staff.

In the winter of 1933–1934, Albright and his staff set out in a caravan of small automobiles (such as Fords and Chevrolets) from Jerusalem to excavate at the site of Ader in Transjordan. Anne H. Fuller, a somewhat headstrong young woman at the American School in Jerusalem, resolved to force her way onto the staff of the expedition. She stowed away in the last car of the caravan and, on reaching Ader, informed Albright that she was on his expedition. Dumbstruck, he came to me and asked what he should do. I advised him to make whatever adjustments were absolutely necessary and then act as though nothing had happened. So Albright rented a small room in a nearby building for Anne, where he escorted her every night after the evening meal. After bidding her good night, he would return to the rest of the staff, where it was tacitly agreed to turn a blind eye to Anne's rashness and behave as though everything was normal.

In all honesty, Anne was her own worst enemy academically. While a Ph.D. candidate at the Oriental Institute of the University of Chicago, she had turned in her entire dissertation in blank verse, all without consulting her mentor, Robert Redfield. It was rejected, and so ended her academic career. Anne was, in fact, a whimsical Yankee who in her youth spoke beautiful English with an elegant pronunciation that she had learned from

---

[21] Dorothy Garrod (1892–1968) studied at Cambridge (1913–1916) and under Abbé Breul in Paris. She specialized in digging in caves in northern Palestine, especially on Mount Carmel (1929–1934) and in Lebanon. From 1939 to 1952 she was Disney Professor at Cambridge.

an elderly relative on the Harvard teaching staff. Still, she did not seem to appreciate or understand how her unconventional antics would affect her superiors such as Albright and Redfield. She spent the last decades of her life in Athens. I like to think that Socrates would have appreciated her more than did her American teachers.

Yet another unforgettable character I met in 1933–1934 bore the name of the Reverend Dr. Tipple. One cold December day in 1933 the Reverend Doctor rang the front doorbell of the American School of Oriental Research in Jerusalem (now known as the Albright School). Albright's brother-in-law, William Steinspring of Duke University, was Acting Director at the time, so he welcomed his guest and offered him some tea. Upon learning that Tipple was on his first trip to the Holy Land, Steinspring suggested that they visit the Church of the Holy Sepulchre after they finished their tea. Tipple agreed, but without enthusiasm. Steinspring did not yet know that the Reverend had given up religion, taken to drink instead, and had never regretted the change.

As they walked toward the Damascus Gate, Tipple turned to Steinspring and said, "I hope you will not think ill of me, but this cold Jerusalem air is gnawing at my very bones. I'll have to have something to warm my innards." Steinspring said that he understood, for he had caught a cold some weeks earlier and had nipped it in the bud by drinking a miniature bottle of whiskey purchased for a shilling at a Jewish rum shop on Jaffa Road. Walking on, they reached the Church of the Holy Sepulchre, where Steinspring explained the history and traditions of the Church's various phases. Tipple paid little attention to Steinspring's expert account. At last they entered the small shrine that contains the sarcophagus in which, according to many Eastern Christians, Christ had been interred. In a hushed voice, Steinspring began to detail the background of the shrine and of the sarcophagus of the Savior. But the Reverend could no longer curb his impatience and yelled, "This is all well and good, Dr. Steinspring, but it is not getting us any nearer the rum shop!"

Realizing Tipple's true interest, Steinspring led him briskly toward Jaffa Road and finally to the rum shop. Steinspring asked the proprietor to show them a shilling bottle of whiskey, which the latter promptly produced and laid on the counter. Tipple, however, was not satisfied. "Please, Dr. Steinspring, do not think ill of me, but we retired clergymen have very limited incomes and can't afford to waste money purchasing goods in small quantities." By this time Steinspring fully understood the situation, so he helped Tipple purchase many large bottles with irresistibly attractive labels. A delivery boy loaded this precious cargo onto his coaster and headed for the King David Hotel, where the Reverend Doctor Tipple enjoyed his luxurious room and was not seen again until he departed some days later. I beg the reader not to think ill of the retired clergyman, for does not the Good Book tell us that spirituous drink is what "gladdens gods and men" (Judg 9:13)?

As I previously noted, tragic events in Iraq prevented us from returning to excavate Tell Billa and Tepe Gawra in 1933–1934. Specifically, in the summer of 1933, the Assyrian Christians, along with several other anti-Baghdad groups had rebelled against government forces. The Iraqi army struck back mercilessly and eventually put down the rebellion, but the situation was so unsettled that it would have been unwise, if not quite impossible, to return. In light of this situation, the American Schools of Oriental Research decided to assign the 1933–1934 Baghdad School's fieldwork budget to Nelson Glueck so he could explore Transjordan and Sinai in the spring of 1934.

Glueck himself broke the news to me that I would assist him in his projected surveys in Moab, Edom, Sinai, and the Negev. Since Glueck was not an epigrapher but rather hoped to map the numerous mounds in the area and date them by the potsherds found on their surface, I asked him whether he would assign to me the publication of any inscriptions that we might find. He snapped back that I would have no share in any publications. Uncowed, I expressed my knee-jerk reaction to the effect that I had plenty of research and writing to do on my own and that I had no desire to be a second-class member of his expedition. Glueck countered with two compelling arguments. If I stayed behind, it might convey the impression at headquarters in Philadelphia that there was friction between us. Furthermore, if I joined the expedition, I would gain valuable archaeological experience.

Eventually I agreed to join Glueck so as to make the most of a less-than-happy situation. I knew that Speiser did not want me to continue at the Baghdad School and that any friendship Montgomery might have for me at headquarters was no match for Speiser's firm resolve to undo me. Academia is so full of such mischief that it is not really of great interest. Glueck and Speiser were in different ways able men who have left a legacy to future generations. Whether or not I enjoyed all of my many dealings with them is of little moment.

At any rate, in April 1934, at the height of spring, when for a few weeks even the desert is in flower, Glueck and I left Jerusalem and headed for Transjordan to begin an archaeological survey of ancient Edom and Moab. Glueck's work proved valuable in providing the history of occupation at many specific sites as well as in the entire region. Glueck made various mistakes, to be sure, and certain aspects of the chronology he proposed had to be modified in the light of later discoveries. Still, Glueck's contributions far outweigh his errors, and we are all indebted to his pioneering work in this field.

Our primary exploratory goal was to examine the surface ruins of Moab and Edom, particularly the numerous mounds within the region, in order to date the occupational periods for each mound and for the region as a whole. Glueck and I had been trained in the dating of Palestinian ceramics and thus could assign the then-accepted dates to ancient pots as well as to certain fragments such as rims, bases, handles, and the like.

Specifically, we would locate each mound on the best map available to us and assign to it an identifying name and/or number. Then we would assemble a large selection of characteristic sherds from the surface and the immediate vicinity of each mound, and tie them up in a labeled cloth bag. On the basis of the ceramic evidence collected at the mounds, we hoped to establish both the occupational periods for each mound and for the region as a whole. Indeed, after visiting and studying approximately five hundred sites, we developed a perception of the area as a whole in its various stages of development.

Surface finds also revealed other significant data. At many sites near copper-bearing quarries, for example, we found groups of smelting ovens with heaps of slag alongside them. This indicated that the inhabitants of this region engaged in copper extraction during the periods that corresponded to the potsherds near the ovens.

The region was sparsely populated in 1934 (the influx of Palestinian refugees would come later), and the entire population was tribally organized and respectful of the principle of a common law. So, though virtually every man had a rifle slung over his shoulder, Transjordan was not lawless. Tribal law and custom prevailed, so strangers such as ourselves would be safe as long as we operated within the rules of tribal law and custom. To that end, we hired camels and camel-boys at the Transjordanian town of Kerak, site of a stronghold during the Crusader period and center of the most powerful tribe of the region. We thereby made ourselves protégés of that tribe, and anyone who killed, injured, or robbed us would bring on his own tribe dire retribution from the tribe in whose care we had entrusted ourselves. As a result, we were able to sleep on the ground in sleeping bags without fear.

In addition to Glueck and me, our expedition staff included an Englishman named Reginald Head, the black-sheep son of an Anglican priest. In the days of the Empire, sons deemed unsuitable for "respectable" British society were often sent to the overseas territories and colonies. Such was the case with Head. After his arrival, Head had joined the Transjordanian police force; by 1934 he had been assigned to the Department of Antiquities, which led to his eventual involvement with our expedition.

The final member of our staff was Ali Abu-Ghosh, an Arab policeman who had been assigned to guard us. He had a sterling character, and the three of us welcomed him as a valued colleague. As a rule he chose to eat his meals with the camel-boys. This proved useful for all concerned, because it provided him with local news that we otherwise might not have known.

Glueck had recently married Helen Iglauer of Cincinnati, a young physician with whom he was deeply in love and whom he keenly missed. One evening he, Head, and I were sitting around the fire on which our supper was being cooked. Our camels, grazing on the desert plants, had one leg hobbled so they could not wander too far. Of us three, I was the only bachelor free to enjoy the experience of exploring a fascinating land without feeling concern for a spouse left behind.

Head often spoke of having his wife join him in Transjordan, but every time he received a paycheck at headquarters in Amman, he retired to the bar at the Hotel Philadelphia (for in the Greco-Roman period, Amman was the Philadelphia of the Decapolis), and went on a binge until his pay was gone. But as we watched the fire that night, Head went into an ecstatic tribute to his wife back in England, a nurse who was quite able to support and take care of herself. Head told us that, back in England, whenever he went out for the evening with his cronies and came home crawling through the gate on his hands and knees, he would scratch at the door to be let in. His wife, well aware that it was not the cat, would help him get into bed and would not say a word about it the next morning.

When Head had finished his tribute, Glueck offered an eloquent encomium to his own wife. He ended by declaring, "If ever I should do anything reprehensible, I would get down on my knees and beg for her forgiveness." Head, disgusted with Glueck's abject "unmanliness," exclaimed, "You should be ashamed of yourself. No real man gets down on his knees to a woman!" Glueck retorted, "Who are you to talk? Only a few minutes ago you admitted that many a time you came home on your knees to your wife!" But that night Head would have the last word: "How dare you compare yourself to me! You would get down on your knees; I rose to mine!" Such was life in the field in the mid-1930s.

Our archaeological surveys, of which there were two in 1934, included Nabatea, where I encountered the most impressive ancient site my eyes have ever seen: the caravan city of Petra, capital of the Nabateans. At Petra nature and art combine to create what a poet has described as "the rose red city half as old as time." Further description of Petra and the significance of Nabatean civilization are not essential to this autobiography. However, I should say something about the gifted woman who identified Nabatean pottery: Agnes Conway. This daughter of Lord Conway was married to George Horsefield, the Director of Antiquities in Transjordan, but she was an accomplished archaeologist in her own right. It was she who identified the thin and delicate painted ware strewn all over Petra as Nabatean. On the basis of her work, one could safely identify as Nabatean other sites where such pottery was present.

The Nabateans understood how to utilize the limited water resources of their dry area so as to grow enough crops to support their population. I might add that what our investigations revealed has been put to practical use in Israel and Jordan today. On the eve of the Arab invasion and conquest of Palestine in the seventh century C.E., not only the Nabateans but also the Byzantine rulers of the country had settlers who knew how to conserve the sparse rains and thus support life in the arid Negev. The American Colt Expedition at Sbeita, for example, revealed the remains of a Byzantine monastic community that had constructed its site so that the rainfall would be funneled into waterproofed cisterns. The excavators cleared away the debris that filled the long abandoned cisterns as well as the dirt that had accumulated over the site. When that particular season, in contrast to the normally dry years, brought a torrential rain that filled the cisterns, the expedition staff had an abundant supply of water for all its needs. Had the archaeologists been so inclined, they could have grown crops, just as the Byzantine monks who first built the monastery centuries earlier had done. We have much of practical value to learn from the past.

Unlike the Byzantine monks and some of their Arabian contemporaries, such as the cultivators of the oases and the South Arabs of fertile Yemen, the seventh century Arab conquerors were not agriculturalists. They were a pastoral people whose cattle grazed and, worse yet, whose goats browsed and grazed, consuming the ground cover and giving saplings no chance to grow. Indeed, humans have the capacity to convert deserts into gardens and gardens into deserts.

In the end, our survey of Edom, Moab, and the Negev attracted wide attention. Glueck's interpretation of the material we had gathered included some errors, to be sure, but such is inevitably the case in pioneer work. Glueck was rudely taken to task for these mistakes by an intellectually gifted but merciless photographer, Benno Rothenburg. However, Albright stood behind his disciple so that Glueck survived the assaults of his critics.

My final year in archaeological fieldwork with the Baghdad School (1934–1935) was devoted once again to excavating at Tepe Gawra and Tell Billa simultaneously. This time our headquarters were located at Fadhiliyya near Gawra. The inhabitants were Bezhwanis: Muslims who understood Arabic but at home spoke a Kurdish dialect. Fethi, our foreman, was intelligent and quickly grasped the principles of field archaeology, such as stratigraphy and typology. He kept after the laborers and saw to it that they worked methodically and with care.

To be sure, Fethi used his position to secure preferential treatment for family members, but this was not unexpected. So we granted Fethi, who had two wives, permission to hire a brother-in-law to guard the mound and its equipment against theft when work was not going on, such as at night or on Sundays, our weekly day off.

One Saturday night, however, a family fight broke out in Fethi's house, in the course of which he and his brother-in-law exchanged blows. The next morning, a Sunday, Fethi asked me to fire his brother-in-law. I replied that I could not accede to this request unless his brother-in-law was remiss in his duties. The only step I could take was to drive out to the mound with Fethi to check on his brother-in-law's work. Apparently the fight had exhausted the brother-in-law, for we caught him fast asleep on the mound. I woke him up and explained that guards were not permitted to sleep on the job. "Thieves could have stolen expensive equipment while you slept. You are fired." Fethi, a believing Muslim, turned his eyes skyward and praised our Heavenly Father: "Allah khosh Ilah!" ("Allah is a good god"). Was not the slumber of the crestfallen guard a miraculous answer to Fethi's prayers?

Within a few days, however, Fethi realized that the loss of the brother-in-law's job meant a reduction in the family income and asked me to reinstate him to his former position. I refused, but as a sop to Fethi's pride, I permitted the brother-in-law's reemployment at the reduced rank and pay of a common laborer.

Back in the States

The prospect of facing a blank future was the sword of Damocles that hung over my head in the spring of 1935. Speiser was determined to destroy me, but Albright, who did not like Speiser, intervened on my behalf. Albright informed Speiser that he would not demand the firing of Speiser's minion, Charles Bache, if Speiser would but lighten up on me. Albright's resolve to take me under his wing resulted in my academic survival for the next three years as a teaching fellow in his department at Johns Hopkins University (1935–1938).

Before my appointment as Albright's assistant, however, I was informed that, although my position in the American School at Baghdad was being terminated, I would be honored with the title of the first "Albert T. Clay Fellow," without salary. No doubt the politically correct response would have been to accept this "honor" with a diplomatic letter of feigned thanks. However, I regarded the whole affair as a "first-class burial" and never dignified the empty honor with a reply.

Curiously enough, my appointment at Johns Hopkins led to a gratifying honor over half a century later. In 1991 Johns Hopkins University (JHU) elected me to its Society of Scholars, a kind of honorary nonalumni association. To be eligible, one must have earned degrees elsewhere, completed post-doctoral research at JHU, and then moved on to other institutions to gain distinction and recognition in one's field.

Not surprisingly, the other 1991 inductees were scientists, particularly those working in some branch of medicine. This rather worked to my advantage, for there were so many honorees in medicine that they seemed routine and evoked rather perfunctory appreciation, and this in spite of the fact that these individuals had made noteworthy advances in brain surgery, noninvasive procedures, cancer therapy, and the like. However, when my faculty sponsor, the JHU Assyriologist, Jerrold S. Cooper, read his account of my accomplishments as the author of the first comprehensive grammar of Ugaritic, decipherer of Minoan, first American cryptanalyst of encoded and enciphered messages in Arabic, Persian, and Turkish, the applause was thunderous. I was the only humanist among the honorees, so my work was hailed enthusiastically. The seemingly ubiquitous medical advances, on the other hand, were taken for granted at JHU. Needless to say, it is not often that a humanist is made to feel so good in our age of scientific technology.

My years at Johns Hopkins were fruitful in several ways. I was near Albright, who was always ready to drop whatever he was doing and listen to any colleague or student with an idea to share. His door was always ajar, and I often barged in to share some new discovery or idea. At such times Albright would, without delay, offer an opinion as well as words of encouragement. Then he would immediately return to what he had been doing before the interruption. If I could be enriched by one of his many remarkable gifts, it would be his ability to recover promptly from interruptions and return to work as though one had never left it.

At Johns Hopkins I taught Akkadian, Hebrew, and the glyptic art of Near East cylinder and stamp seals. In my language and literature classes, I began to point out organic parallels between pre-Hellenistic Greek literature and ancient Near Eastern literatures. Ultimately my observations led to the writing of *The Common Background of Greek and Hebrew Civilizations*, in which I concluded that the two, far from being poles apart, were parallel structures built upon the same East Mediterranean foundation.

A further by-product of this insight was my decipherment of Minoan as a Northwest Semitic dialect, which constituted an important specific channel of transmission. In my work on Minoan Linear A (and on Ugaritic), I learned that there is a great difference between translating a known language and deciphering an unknown one. If, while reading an English document, we do not know what the word *cool* means, we simply look it up in a dictionary. If, however, we are reading a Minoan Linear A tablet that lists six men and then ends with the word *kull,* which is pronounced much like English *cool,* followed by the number six, the probable meaning of *kull* is "total." As a matter of fact, there are so many totals in the Minoan tablets, all of them preceded by *kull,* that we may safely conclude that *kull* means "total." This conclusion is further substantiated by the fact that *kull,* the common Semitic word for "all," actually appears before a total in the Hebrew Bible (Josh 12:24), precisely as in Minoan.

Similarly, one can conclude that the Minoan word *yan* (written syllabically *ya-na*) means "wine" because it is inscribed on one of a group of wine jars found together in the excavations of Knossos. All the other jars in the ensemble bear the ideogram for "wine," so it is safe to conclude that *ya-na* likewise means "wine." In addition, I did not hesitate to identify Minoan *ya-na* with *yay(i)n* (Hebrew for "wine") in spite of the absence of the second *y*. A decipherer must not be stymied by little surprises. It turns out that the reduction of the diphthong *ay* to *a* is common in the Aegean region. The reduction is also familiar in Hebrew from the silent *y* in words such as *ba-nay-hu* "his sons" (pronounced *banaw*). Minoan Linear A is, to be sure, related to Hebrew, but the decipherer must not conclude that it is identical with Hebrew. Indeed, Ugaritic, Hebrew, Aramaic, Phoenician, and various Canaanite dialects all belong to the Northwest subdivision of the Semitic languages. But there is bound to be new data that we do not expect, so we must remain open to all options, as I was when I first began to recognize the common background of the Hebrew and Greek civilizations.

My preoccupation with seals was based on my possession of photographs of impressions taken of the collection in the Iraq Museum. The photographs were a helpful teaching tool, and I illustrated various classroom lectures with them. I also found, at the Walters Art Gallery in Baltimore, a previously unknown collection of seals, which I published in the journal *Iraq* in 1939. One of these seals, dating from approximately 1300 B.C.E., depicts two men riding a Bactrian camel, a fact that has some bearing on the mention of camels in Genesis.

At that time Albright was making a big issue of the mention of camels in the patriarchal narratives, insisting that it was all an anachronism. In reality, Albright hated camels and did not want to "contaminate" the patriarchs with them. This was one of several developments that soured my relations with Albright. He saw in me a threat, not to his reputation or influence, but to particular pet theories of his. It was during this period that I made the painful discovery that many persons of outstanding scholarship and ability often have a certain, serious flaw. When the chips are down and their pet theories are negated by the facts, they try to conceal their mistakes through oratory and appeals to their reputation. They are not so much interested in the truth as in protecting a legacy. As one who had dedicated his life to seeking the truth, I mistakenly assumed that the leading scholars in the field shared this commitment.

In spite of my growing disenchantment with Albright, I recognized a number of fine qualities in him. For example, Albright helped a number of Jewish refugees from Nazi Germany, giving them temporary positions in his department. One of these individuals was Georg Steindorff, a grand old man with an impressive record in Egyptology. Steindorff's Coptic studies remain valuable, and his edition of the Baedecker Guide to Egypt is still the best for ancient sites. While in Baltimore, he discovered an important but then unknown Egyptological collection stored away in crates at the Walters Art Gallery. Steindorff also published the Catalogue of the Walters Collection, so that the latter is now the fifth largest known Egyptological collection in the western hemisphere, ranking only behind the collections at the Metropolitan Museum in New York, the University Museum in Philadelphia, the Boston Museum of Fine Art, and the Brooklyn Museum.

Albright's attitude toward me was steadily deteriorating, so I decided to leave Baltimore in 1938. I shall specify only one of the manifestations of that change for the worse. For some years Albright had been working closely with H. L. Ginsberg and me.[22] The closeness of this working relationship was particularly noticeable in articles that each of us wrote for *BASOR,* which Albright edited. Albright was far more original than most scholars, but he was somewhat tied to both religious and academic consensus. In early 1938 I submitted to him, for publication in *BASOR,* articles that diverged from positions he had taken in some of his previous articles. My evidence was sound, and, with impolitic naiveté, I assumed he would welcome the progress I had made. Instead, he turned red with anger. So, rather than try to placate him, I decided to leave Baltimore to accept a lectureship at Smith College, where my main function would be the publication of the Smith College collection of cuneiform tablets, though I would also be expected to teach ancient history and biblical Hebrew there.

---

[22] Ginsberg was born in Montreal, Canada, and received the Ph.D. in Semitics at the University of London, afterward spending several years in Palestine. He did some of the early work on the Ugaritic tablets. Ginsberg was the first to offer accurate translations of entire sentences in Ugaritic. He later served as a professor at the Jewish Theological Seminary.

4.
EARLY TEACHING CAREER

My departure from Johns Hopkins was, on the surface, amicable and had not led to a complete break with Albright. It had been obvious to me for some time that, although Albright respected my ability, he would never allow me to attain a condign academic position. Unlike Speiser, he did not try to destroy me, but merely to keep me on "unilateral respiration." I will never fully understand why anyone would behave so misanthropically, least of all a scholar of Albright's stature. There are many realities in life that we must recognize without fully knowing the reasons why. Genesis 6:5–6 addresses this dilemma by stating that God himself admitted he had made a bad job in his creation of humans: "Yahweh saw that great was the evil of humans in the land, and the inclination of the thoughts of their hearts was only evil all day. So Yahweh regretted that he had made humans in the land, and he was sick at heart." Perhaps the best we can do is to recognize the existence of evil and to do what we can to rise above it.

Smith College was socially congenial but academically unstimulating, in spite of the presence of several excellent scholars on the faculty. Deane Montgomery, for one, was an outstanding mathematician who turned down an invitation to Harvard because he disliked the head of the mathematics department there. Montgomery later joined the Yale faculty but was not happy there either. Finally he was called to be a professor at the world's finest department of mathematics: the Institute for Advanced Study in Princeton, New Jersey, where he felt at home and where, after many years of distinguished service, he retired. Montgomery and I became friends at Smith and continued our friendship later at Princeton. I have always felt more at home intellectually with mathematicians and scientists than with humanists. In my view, the former are more inclined to follow the facts and are less subjective than most humanists. This preference continues to the present, for, as a Fellow of the American Academy of Arts and Sciences, I am closer to my science colleagues than to the scholars in the humanities.

My memories of Smith College include my stay as a boarder in the home of an elderly widow, Mrs. Manson. In those days I was often invited to cocktail parties, of which there were many, at the college. Mrs. Manson, who had been raised as a teetotaling Methodist, did not approve of this, but she never upbraided me. One Sunday afternoon, however, after I returned from a cocktail party, Mrs. Manson greeted me with the news that she had just entertained some ladies of the church, who had inquired about the young man living in her house. She informed them that I taught Bible and religion at the college. Among church people in a college town, teaching Bible and religion at "The College" is an awesome and revered role. The spokeswoman of the delegation exclaimed, "Mrs. Manson, you are the luckiest woman in the world to be living under the same roof with a man of God!" When I inquired about her reply, Mrs. Manson retorted with undiluted frankness, "To tell the truth, I didn't say nothin'. I thought it was just as well to let those good women go on thinking that you were a man of God."

I also recall the day when, as I sat copying tablets, the college librarian, Mary Dunham, called on me to seek my advice on renewing the fire insurance policies for the various collections in the library. She wanted to know specifically whether the tablets should be insured for a higher figure than they currently were. She was surprised when I advised her to cancel all the fire insurance on the tablets because burning would only bake them hard as brick and preserve them better than ever. That the cuneiform tablets were the only documents in the Smith Library that fire could not destroy spread to the amazement of the college community.

At the end of that academic year (1938–1939), I still had another year at Smith scheduled and funded for finishing my project. Then an unexpected letter came in the mail. Back in 1927 I had applied to The American-Scandinavian Foundation for a fellowship to study in Sweden. My application had been turned down but kept on file. In 1939, however, when talk of war in Europe was in the air and American students were in no hurry to travel to Europe, I was finally offered a fellowship to Sweden.

By this time I had become more "street wise" in the workings of academia. I was guaranteed a second year at Smith, but I did not want to wait until that year was finished to find my next appointment. With this in mind, I had applied for a membership in the Institute for Advanced Study at Princeton to gain another year of grace. My primary scholarly interest at that time was to write a comprehensive Ugaritic grammar. Ugaritic, however, was a pioneering subject, and no fellowship committee had ever heard of nor would be likely to support such a then-unknown quantity. So I submitted as my subject "The Miniature Glyptic Art of the Ancient Near East." My monograph on the seals in the Walter's Art Gallery was already in proof, so I would be able to submit it as evidence of my research in the field. Ernst Herzfeld was a professor at the Institute, and I welcomed the chance to be under his wing. He is one of the great polymaths with whom I have had the privilege of working. At any rate, I was awarded the membership at the Institute for 1939–1940, and Smith College deferred my second year there till 1940–1941. I had become expert in the art of survival in the academic jungle, pending the hour of professional salvation: a real academic position with tenure.

In light of these plans, I accepted the Scandinavian-American fellowship with the understanding that it would be a 1939 summer award, extending only from June to September. Knowing that the committee would only be confused with Ugaritic as my project, I submitted glyptic art as my topic and received an award of $500 to work at Uppsala. In those days when the dollar went far, this paid for a round-trip trans-Atlantic steamer fare and for living in Sweden for three months, plus a trip by rail from Stockholm to Oslo, Norway, through the spectacular fjord country between Trondheim to Oslo. I was in Oslo when the Second World War broke out on September 3, 1939. There was a panic among the Americans visiting Norway at that time to get some sort of passage home. Luckily, I had prearranged passage on the attractive Norwegian ship, the *Oslofjord*.

My stay in Scandinavia was both productive and enjoyable. At the University of Uppsala, I wrote the first draft of the *Ugaritic Grammar,* which appeared in 1940 and established my reputation as a scholar. I also spent the evenings and vacation days with medical students, during the course of which I learned to speak Swedish fluently. It was also my first and only taste of university campus life, because I had lived at home while taking all my degrees at the University of Pennsylvania. In fact, I enjoyed every minute of my stay in Sweden, including the three months of living in the university dormitory as a typical student.

The academic standards in Sweden back in 1939 were higher than those then current in America. A few of the older students in the humanities, in addition to knowing their areas of specialization, enjoyed speaking to each other in Latin. The typical Swedish citizen possessed only a grade-school education, but even this training enabled most to read with ease, to write effectively and neatly, and to apply arithmetical procedures accurately.

The people of Sweden also took pride in the quality of their workmanship. In the beautiful Uppsala cemetery (*kirkogård*), I was struck by the tombstones that gave the deceased titles such as *Mästerskomakare* ("Master Shoemaker"). This reflected not the values of modern unionism but the old hereditary pride of the guilds. Alas, those pre-World War II virtues were rarely part of the closing years of the twentieth century.

In late September 1939, after my summer fellowship in Sweden, I moved to Princeton to begin my research and writing at the Institute for Advanced Study. I called on Herzfeld, gave him a reprint of my descriptive catalogue of the seals in the Walter's Art Gallery, and described for him my current work on the *Ugaritic Grammar*. Much to my delight, he assured me that I was free to work on any topic I considered important.

The director of the Institute was the person who had conceived it: Abraham Flexner. He had been inspired by the standards of Johns Hopkins to establish a think tank staffed permanently by great scientists and scholars, with temporary appointments of younger members who would be enabled to perform research and prepare it for publication in a tranquil atmosphere without administrative or teaching commitments. Every afternoon the Institute held an optional tea party, where professors and members socialized and engaged in private conversations. There was no agenda. The intellectual giants whom younger scholars might meet included Albert Einstein and John von Neuman. Ernst Herzfeld, who was the only Orientalist at the Institute, rarely attended the tea party, but he always welcomed me to visit him in his sumptuous office, a museum full of his private collection of choice antiquities.

Like every member of the Institute, I had a private office where I could work whenever I wished, night or day. The thick wooden office door had no window, so I enjoyed complete privacy without interference or disturbance. Mercifully, there was no phone.

In such an idyllic academic setting, it is not surprising that my first year at the Institute (1939–1940) proved to be enormously productive. In order to compose a reliable Ugaritic grammar/manual/textbook, I would need to base every detail on correctly translated texts. At that time, H. L. Ginsberg, whose knowledge of the Hebrew Bible was phenomenal, offered the best Ugaritic interpretations and translations. However, the field as a whole was chaotic, with authors translating as they pleased.

To provide the data for my work, I recorded each correctly translated passage on a three-by-five-inch slip of paper and placed it in a shoebox. In time I created thousands of such slips. The advantage of working in this manner was simple. The slips of paper could be rearranged as I formulated each section and subsection of my opus: the parts of speech (e.g., nouns, verbs), inflections (e.g., verb tenses and moods; nominatives, accusatives, genitives), syntax, vocabulary, and so on.

Once I had written the material, I faced yet another challenge. Clearly, I would need to refer to a variety of Semitic languages in order to establish the meanings of the Ugaritic vocabulary, but identifying those languages typographically might easily become cumbersome. There are also many loanwords in Ugaritic, because it was written in an age of internationalism (the Amarna Age, ca. 1400–1200 B.C.E.). Therefore, Hurrian and other exotic languages would have to be cited. Luckily, the German Jesuit scholars of the Pontificium Institutum Biblicum could cope with all the complexities of the problem. Their typograhy made it possible to indicate all the various languages (e.g., Syriac, Ethiopic, hieroglyphic Egyptian, Coptic, South Arabic) simply by using the correct ancient script. If I had not been working with the Pontificium Institutum Biblicum, I might never have found another publisher able to produce my *Ugaritic Grammar*. In all probability, it would have remained unpublished.

The Institute for Advanced Study enabled me to finish the typescript of the book, to correct the proofs, and to return them via papal diplomatic pouch so that the book was published and distributed internationally in 1940. The positive reception that the book received confirmed my credentials as a scholar. Yet my Jewish heritage made it most unlikely that I would ever secure a tenured position in a non-Jewish university such as Harvard, Yale, or Princeton.

Anti-Semitism is forever with us, though it takes on different forms with the passing of time. I believe that there is a special reason why it has been particularly strong in Christianity since at least the third century C.E. Jesus was born a Jew and died a Jew. He preached in synagogues, and in the tradition of the Old Testament prophets, scolded the people for their shortcomings rather than praised them for their virtues. His sermons were strictly in-house messages, not for the ears of non-Jews. But after the death of Jesus, Paul and his successors spread the doctrine of salvation through faith in Christ among the Gentiles, who had no background in the Old Testament. The Gentiles took the scoldings in the synagogue sermons of Jesus out of context (as Krister Stendahl has pointed out) and viewed the Jews as archvillains. The origins of anti-Semitism lie, in short, both in a misunderstanding of Jews and in a misinterpretation of Jesus.

Max Nordau (1849–1923) shrewdly observed that the faults of Jews are not the cause of anti-Semitism; rather, anti-Semitic tendencies cause people to look for faults they can attribute to Jews. I remember the days when Jews were accused of having all the money in the world, and the Arabs had nothing. But when Arabia, the Gulf States, and Iraq were found to be "floating on oil," the Arabs had all the money. Virtually everyone else was broke and indebted to the Arabs. Similarly, Jews had long been regarded as cowards, but when they defeated the invading armies of Egypt, Jordan, Saudi Arabia, Iraq, Syria, and Lebanon, who were united in their dedication to destroy Israel, Jews were suddenly accused of being ruthless warriors. Jews were also accused of eating the food produced by Gentiles, while producing no food themselves. Then Israel became an exporter of food, so the anti-Semites found other accusations. And so it goes on and on, ad infinitum. The anti-Semites never tire of looking for Jewish faults.

When I embarked on my academic career, a "gentlemen's agreement" kept Jews out of tenure-track positions so that they would not become too influential in the universities. Sad to say, I once encountered this prejudice face to face at a meeting of the American Oriental Society in Philadelphia. I was in the restroom when A. T. Olmstead of the Oriental Institute of the University of Chicago came in and remarked to Sterling Dow of Harvard, "I saw you talking to Cyrus Gordon, and I must tell you that he is a fine

Jewish scholar" emphasizing the word *Jewish*. Later, when Olmstead became aware of my presence and realized that I had overheard his comment, he tried to cover up his mischief by telling me, "I have the highest regard for Jewish scholarship and was recommending you in the highest terms to Sterling Dow."

By the end of the Second World War, however, Jewish scholars finally began to be appointed to tenured positions. The ultimate cause of this change was that the reputation of universities depended largely on the research and publications of their faculties. One incident that took place during the mid-forties at M.I.T. will illustrate what was happening. A professor at the Technion in Haifa, Israel, was on the advisory council of M.I.T., and the president of M.I.T. asked him what could be done to make the faculty more productive in research and publication. His reply was brief and to the point: "Hire Jews." Pressing on, the president asked: "What proportion of the Jews we appoint can we count on to do research and publish, 30 percent?" Again the reply was brief and to the point: "No, 100 percent!"

History demonstrates that Jews who enter university service as a member of the faculty will engage in research and publication because that is what they want to do. Business and financial success are necessary for a community to thrive, but intellectual achievement wins more respect among Jews. If a Jew has two children, one a wealthy businessperson and the other a scholarly professor, that parent will generally be most proud of the latter. Because of this esteem for scholarship, the American intellectual elite became predominantly Jewish between 1920 and 1970. Now other minorities, especially those of East Asian extraction, are making their own steady inroads.

To return to 1940, however, finishing the *Ugaritic Grammar* provided me with time to call on a few Princeton scholars who had not put in an appearance at the Institute. Of these, the first I visited was Harold Bender. When I called him on the phone to request a meeting, he invited me to call on him at tea time, which I did. When we met, I told Bender how highly my teacher, Roland Kent,[23] had spoken of his scholarship and how interesting I had found his book on the home of the Primitive Indo-Europeans. Bender thanked me for the compliments, then asked what favor I had come to ask. I assured him that my visit was prompted only by a desire to meet him, that I had absolutely no favor to ask. To my embarrassment, he did not believe me. I reassured him that there was no favor he could bestow, for I had a generously endowed membership at the Institute and was at the height of a productive career. At last, convinced

---

[23] Roland Kent taught comparative philology and Indo-European Culture at the University of Pennsylvania. He also taught Old Persian, which I studied with him. He was a founding father of the Linguistic Institute of America.

that I had no boon to request of him, he said, "This is the first time in my life that anyone has called on me without wanting a favor."

I had already spent a decade of my life in postdoctoral professional teaching, field archaeology, research, and publication, yet I had not obtained a tenure-track position. Little did I realize that those years of financial and professional insecurity enabled me to build up the foundation (as reflected in an extensive bibliography) of a long and successful career.

During 1940–1941 I completed my two-year stint at Smith College, devoting myself primarily to making autographed copies of 110 cuneiform tablets in the Smith College Collection. Eventually, in 1952, they were published as a volume in the Smith College Historical series. During this year I also taught biblical Hebrew and the history of Greece and Rome. But with the specter of war on the horizon, my life was soon to undergo a significant change.

5.
WORLD WAR II

As a Cryptanalyst

A few months after I returned to the Institute for the 1941–1942 academic year, the attack on Pearl Harbor (December 7, 1941) catapulted the United States into World War II. Unbeknownst to me, there was a sudden need for cryptanalysts to break the codes and the ciphers that nations were using to send secret messages, which we (or anyone else) could intercept out of the airwaves. The cryptanalyst recruiting center was located at Fort Monmouth, in the vicinity of nearby Red Bank, New Jersey. Naturally, the recruiting personnel turned to the Institute for qualified people with background in languages and/or mathematics.

I had majored in math during high school and the first half of my college years. Thereafter, I had specialized not merely in languages but also in working out the structures, vocabulary, and translation of problematic languages such as Ugaritic. In short, I was qualified for the job. But for the sensitive work of cryptanalysis, I also needed a top-secret clearance, which required months of investigation. As I awaited the completion of the investigation, I went to Washington, D.C., in March or April 1942 to work as a civilian in the Army cryptanalysis center. There I hoped to learn as much about the field as possible before entering official service. During that time, I not only worked with the Japanese, German, and weather sections but also studied, in the evenings, the excellent correspondence courses prepared by the great cryptanalyst, Col. William Friedman of the Army Signal Corps. Finally, in July 1942, the investigation was completed, and I was inducted as an officer in the Signal Corps of the United States Army, the very same division in which Friedman served.

Among the skills I had to learn was how to use the IBM computers, primitive machines by today's computers. A punch card was prepared for each item. Then the computer would sort and print the data as specified. For example, an encoded and/or enciphered intercepted message from London would presumably be in English. So if a particular five-digit group (e.g., 38510) occurred frequently but only initially or medially, never at the end of a message, one could infer that it was *and, a,* or, more probably, *the*.

Japanese, unlike English, is an agglutinative language that employs suffixes. One common suffix, *-wa,* also happens to be the most common syllable in Japanese. So, by calculating the frequency and placement of various sequences, we would be able to deduce what the code or cipher stood for. Then, once we had established the phonetic value of a sequence of syllables, we would call in someone who knew the Japanese language to translate it, if possible. Tragically, we did not trust any of our own Japanese citizens, in contrast to the way we trusted most of our citizens of German or Italian extraction, so we had to rely on approximately twenty white citizens who knew Japanese sufficiently well and who could be cleared for top-secret work. Nearly all of our translators came from missionary families who had spent considerable time in Japan. Professor Edwin Reischauer of Harvard was the most distinguished of them. On a more personal note, the cryptanalytic methods that I had learned proved to be of value in my research after the war, particularly in the decipherment of Minoan Linear A and the allied dialects and scripts in the Aegean sphere.

Our cryptanalysts did much to win the war. They cracked the Japanese naval code and could read messages as quickly as the Japanese cryptographers could. Accordingly, if a Japanese submarine was ordered to a specific spot at a specific time, American planes or ships would go there in time to destroy it. Recognizing the advantage that we had, we changed the key to our encipherments fairly often. The Japanese, however, kept the same key, never realizing that we had no trouble promptly converting their enciphered messages into plain text.

On the other hand, although we intercepted many messages from the Middle East countries, our cryptanalytic agencies did little or nothing with them. During World War II the United States emphasized other areas, such as Japan, Germany, and the Soviet Union. The British, however, who possessed both good personnel and experience in Middle Eastern affairs, actively sought information about what was taking place in the region. Granted, they would usually share their knowledge with us, if we requested as much, but they did not want us to have the capability to work independently of them.

As an American, I felt that we should not be dependent on our British ally. I shall always regard the United Kingdom as, if not our "mother country," then at least our "grandmother country," but I viewed our indifference to the Middle East as a serious mistake. When, however, I suggested that our outfit establish a Middle East section, I encountered strong opposition. Still I persisted in making the case for founding a section to handle the systems of countries using the Arabic script. My opponents sent delegations in order to learn whatever I knew so that they could steal my thunder. I thought that my knowledge of the Middle East languages was what they wanted, but my linguistic competence carried little weight with them. They were accustomed to depending on dictionaries. (They did not understand that, although dictionaries are useful reference books, reliance on them indicates ignorance of a language.) Finally, something that I did not anticipate scared them off. When I innocently revealed that the script of Arabic, Persian, and Ottoman Turkish ran from right to left, they could not accept something so unthinkable, something so foreign to the limited intellectual world in which they lived. They threw up their hands, fled in dismay, and never bothered me again.

In time, I was able to recruit a few people with suitable training to be of some help in cracking the codes and cyphers of Middle East countries such as Iraq, Iran, and Turkey. Messages intercepted from the Egyptians were based on code books in French, for which we had abundant personnel. However, I had to teach the basics of the Middle Eastern languages written in Arabic script so that newcomers would be of some immediate use in our task. Because it was wartime, money was available to secure all the people, books, and other resources that section chiefs requested. So it was that, within a little more than a year, every Middle Eastern code and cipher had been cracked. The strain of the in-fighting and the administrative tensions in Washington had exhausted me, but my achievements gave me great satisfaction, which has only grown with the years. After the war, many of my team elected to remain in cryptanalysis and headed up Middle Eastern sections in various military and civilian agencies of the government.

In the Persian Gulf Command

As soon as I felt that the work of my section could go on without me, I asked for a transfer to overseas service in the Middle East. My own outfit did not want to release me, so I would have to maneuver my escape from the Washington jungle. I did not have to wait long.

Since I was an officer in the Signal Corps, various classified messages routinely crossed my desk. One particular message, from the Persian Gulf Command to the Personnel Office in the Pentagon, gave me my chance for freedom. It had taken the message only a split second to travel from Iran to Washington, but I knew it would take several days for the message to wend its way through the Washington maze before it reached the Personnel Office in the Pentagon. Wasting no time, I took a motor-pool bus to the main Personnel Office, where I casually inquired if there were any openings for officers in the Middle East. I was told there were no openings. I then asked if I might drop in again to check on future developments and was told that I was always welcome. So, when I went back a few days later, the personnel officer greeted me by saying, "You must be psychic! I just received a request for thirty-five officers and five hundred enlistees for the PGC [Persian Gulf Command]. I can't imagine anyone wanting to go to such a hellhole." I explained that I had a professional civilian interest in the Middle East and that I wanted him to sign me up for the PGC. He responded, "If you're crazy enough to want to go, you're first on the list. There's no accounting for taste. Good luck."

Within a few days I was shipped off to a staging area at Shenango in western Pennsylvania. When the officer in charge of the area in which I was billeted asked how I liked the place, I told him that it was balm for a weary soul exhausted from working in Washington, a veritable rest cure. He warned me not to say such things to anyone, but to look busy. Appearing busy when there is nothing to do but wait for one's transport to the port of embarkation is an art for which I have no talent. My "unsoldierly" manner was due in part to the fact that I had been commissioned directly from civilian life and thus had not gone through basic training as a soldier. The Army needed officers like me for their background in languages and mathematics, even if we did not know how to appear busy when there was no work to be done. In fact, my lack of experience with troops plagued me during the months of travel from Hampton Roads, Virginia, to Iran, as will become evident later on.

The ride on the troop train from Shenango to Hampton Roads imposed one simple mission on the officers: to deliver every enlisted man, body and soul, to the port of embarkation. Whenever the train stopped, the officers would get off to make sure no one climbed out of a lavatory window to desert. That was in the autumn of 1942. In the summer of 1945, on the way home, there was no need to keep them from deserting. We simply told them not to wander off lest they get lost and miss the ship homeward bound. There is all the difference in the world between sailing off to war and sailing back home.

Our convoy eastward across the Atlantic consisted of a vast armada of Liberty Ships as well as several airplanes and armed Naval units to defend us against any German submarines that might try to torpedo us. The Liberty Ships also carried depth charges to destroy or ward off submarines. Although I held the same rank as quite a few of the officers on board, I automatically became commander of all thirty-five officers and five hundred men, for I had "more time in grade" (i.e., I had been appointed to that grade before any of the others). They, however, had all been through basic training and had some troop experience.

The ship carried plenty of flour for bread but only enough ovens to bake two slices of bread for each soldier per day. The crew that operated the ship were not military but merchant mariners with more than enough supplies for themselves. Unfortunately, they took shameful advantage of the hungry soldiers and sold them jelly sandwiches for $5 each. This kind of "nature in the raw" was new to me. The ivory tower of academia was not all sweetness and light, but its inhumanity did not include gouging hungry fellow citizens for bread.

To my further dismay, I discovered that, in direct violation of Department of Defense regulations, our troop ship was carrying a cargo of explosives. If we were torpedoed, there would be no survivors to rescue from the sea. When I asked the ship's captain how such a dangerous violation had been committed, he explained nonchalantly, "The Army got a waiver." Waivers in wartime work like indulgences in religion, except that waivers endanger lives, while indulgences merely permit peccadilloes or grant harmless conveniences.

Human folly and inconsistency did not start yesterday or even the day before. They are as old as the human race. Nevertheless, my military experience added greatly to my perspective as a historian. Sherman rightly stated that "War is hell," but any scholar with the good fortune to survive a war unscathed can learn a great deal and emerge a better scholar as well as a wiser person.

My lack of experience with troops kept me from understanding the role of gambling in the life of soldiers. They know that when one individual ends up with all the money, that person is usually a crook who has duped and cheated the rest. It turned out that a gangster named Mickey from my home town of Philadelphia won all the money on board, although he never rolled the dice. He was simply an onlooker who made side bets. Eventually, a street-wise soldier in my battalion discovered the shameful truth. He saw Mickey lending a pair of dice to a player at the start of a game, then noted that Mickey kept winning side bets. Finally he asked to have a look at the dice and noted that they were "six-ace-flats." A thin slice had been cut away from one surface so that the dice were not quite cubical, which conditioned the probable numbers that a throw of the dice would produce.

The rest of the players, of course, became enraged. Gambling was important to them, and they did not like being cheated out of their fun or their money. Soon I caught wind of a plot to throw Mickey overboard. Acting on the urgent and wise advice of a fellow officer with troop experience, I averted the plot by threatening them all with court-martial for manslaughter and imprisonment at Leavenworth, if anyone should be missing. Mickey knew he deserved to be executed, but he was grateful to me for delivering him from vengeance at the hands of his victims. When we finally reached shore and it was time for me to part from my troops, Mickey took me aside and said, "You saved my life. When we get back to civilian life, I want to show my gratitude. Whenever you want someone bumped off, just let me know, and I'll have him rubbed out." Needless to say, I never asked him to return my favor.

The route from Hampton Roads to Iran led us across the Atlantic, through the Straits of Gibraltar, and to Oran, Algeria. There we disembarked and were billeted at Canestel, on a height overlooking the city. We stayed at Canestel several weeks, until transportation was available to take us eastward toward the PGC. By ship we traveled to Port Sa'id and thence by railroad to Cairo, where we were billeted for a month at nearby Camp Huckstep. Since there was no work to perform, I seized the moment to visit antiquity sites and to call on scholars, most notably J. P. Lauer, the foremost authority on Saqqara. (I had the pleasure of meeting him again, still working at the step pyramid, in 1978.)

When it was time to move on, we struck out toward Iran in a motor convoy, stopping first in Baghdad for several days. On our first afternoon in Baghdad, I visited some long-time friends. Sir Edwin Drower was a respected British judge, while Lady E. Stefana Drower, then on her way to becoming the leading authority on the Mandaeans,[24] had been a close friend since my archaeological days in Iraq (1931–1935) and a regular correspondent on Mandaica thereafter. How good to have tea and scones in their parlor, warmed by their British hospitality and their fireplaces. I also enjoyed the luxury of a shower, so welcome a treat after a dusty ride across the desert! The conversation enabled me to catch up on Iraqi affairs and professional developments in the field.

Before sunset, I took my leave and returned to camp, where I found things in turmoil. Iraqi, British, and American military police had taken control of the area in which my troops were encamped. Men in one of my companies had robbed shops in the jewelers' bazaar, and all the loot was found in the barracks bags of my men. There was no doubt as to the identity of the thieves.

I felt embarrassed, particularly because I was known to the archaeologists of Iraq and had many friends such as the Drowers in Baghdad. Instead of brooding over the shameful behavior of my men, I decided to drown my sorrows in work. One of my chores was to censor my battalion's mail. One of the letters I examined that night was from a Brooklyn soldier to his mother. It ran something as follows: "Dear Mom: I can't tell you where I am because it's a military secret, but I can give you a good hint. This place was once famous as the haunt of Ali Baba and the forty thieves. But things have changed. It's now Lt. Gordon and the forty thieves."

What a relief it was when we moved on to Ahwaz, in the Iranian province of Khuzistan. There I bade farewell to my battalion, never again to endure troop duty. Al-hamdu lillah ("Praise be to Allah")!

Khuzistan was congenial to me linguistically. Though it was a province of Iran, most of the population was Arabic and spoke a dialect of Iraq that I could handle with ease. Within a few days, I traveled to Tehran to join

---

[24] Mandaeanism is the last living survival of Gnosticism. In olden times there were gnostic brands of both Judaism and Christianity. Mandaean is a dialect of Aramaic.

the Office of Technical Information, where I dealt with Middle East affairs for the commanding general and his staff. It was a gratifying assignment because it enabled me to broaden my spot-knowledge of the Middle East to include Iran. I learned a great deal from the numerous tours that I took on official missions throughout western Iran, from the Persian Gulf to the Caspian Sea.

As the Allied capital in the Middle East, Tehran was an ideal place to meet the military and civilian elite of Iran, Britain, and the Soviet Union, as well as the entire diplomatic corps. During World War II, the Persian Gulf Command was the only theater of operations in which American and Soviet forces met, and harmoniously at that. We were to supply, in accordance with a lend-lease policy, whatever the Soviets needed to defeat the Germans on the eastern front. The Soviets received and transported the materiel, food, and other supplies to their gallant troops on the German front. The British supplied the security, largely with Sikh and Gurka units serving under British command. The PGC consisted of about thirty thousand American officers and men, whose role in winning the war was significant, though not heroic.

I had studied Old Persian with Roland G. Kent when I was a graduate student, and during my stay in Iran (late 1943 to mid 1945), I read a lot of classical Islamic literature, albeit with the aid of Edward Browne's magisterial four-volume *Literary History of Persia*. I even taught courses in colloquial Persian to PGC soldiers who were interested. Yet I never felt comfortable in colloquial Persian because I lived and worked all day with Americans. I did have more than a modicum of social life off base in Tehran, but my friends there preferred to speak French. At the time, I was still fluent in French, but I would have preferred to speak colloquial Persian.[25]

Among my many Tehran friends was a Russian family named Kozminsky. The parents had escaped Russia during the early days of the revolution and had settled in Iran. Their two daughters, who were born in Iran, spoke Russian at home but Persian with their Iranian friends and neighbors. They also learned French at the Catholic schools they attended.

One of the daughters, named Louba, was very communicative. She introduced me to many of her family and friends and described for me their lifestyles. Her brother-in-law was General Jahanbani (there were two by that name), whose first and older wife was a wealthy Qajar princess. His second wife, Louba's sister, had been fourteen years old when the general had married her. I asked Louba how a middle-aged man such as

---

[25] I began to lose my fluency in speaking a number of languages when I married and settled down in September 1946. I have lived so close a family life that I retained my polyglot skills only by reading. My skill in the latter permeated my classroom instruction throughout my teaching career.

General Jahanbani could marry a fourteen-year-old child. Louba informed me that in Iran "fourteen is the ideal age of women." In reality, the bigamous Jahanbani family worked out well. It did not end up in any divorces. The wives maintained separate homes, and the general alternated between them, one night with one, and the next night with the other. This gave the women time for their own social lives with their female friends, without having to look after a husband on alternate days.

One of Louba's friends was an elegant Russian prince by the name of Romanovsky, a relative of the late Tsar. She asked me to invite him to dinner at the Officers Club so that the hungry prince could enjoy a square meal. I did so, but he took a mere nibble of each dish and explained that he wasn't hungry. Later I told Louba that I did not understand why a starving man did not eat that really delicious dinner. She replied, "Romanovsky was famished, but he did not want you to know it." Such pride does not make for survival. The Russian nobility in Iran, unlike many Russian Jewish refugees, did not do well.

Among Louba's Iranian friends was the Malek-e-Tojjara family. The family founder had been given the title Malek-e-Tojjara ("King of the merchants") by a Qajar Shah. Once Louba and I visited the current head of the family, who lived in a house in the bazaar near the great mosque. This man, known simply as Malek, had three daughters, all of whom had married businessmen and who lived in modern apartments. Walking through the bazaar to the house of Malek posed problems. Our guide was one of the daughters, who had to avoid being seen not only with an American officer in that kind of neighborhood but even with a blue-eyed woman such as Louba. So Louba followed at a safe distance, and I in turn followed Louba at a comparably safe distance. Separately we entered Malek's house.

The furniture was old-fashioned native Iranian. Malek himself was a gracious man of about seventy, whose prized possession consisted of a collection of nearly three thousand Islamic manuscripts, mainly Persian and Arabic. Quite a few were adorned with painted miniature illustrations. Having heard that I was a scholar, he asked me what manuscripts I might like to see. I replied that I would much enjoy viewing illustrated copies of the national epic, Ferdosi's *Shahname* ("The Epic of Kings"). Malek instructed his librarian to show a few to me, and the librarian went to the chest containing the *Shahname* and retrieved a few superb copies, which he placed in my hands. They were indeed choice works of the scribal and miniature painter's arts. The British Museum or the Louvre would have paid millions, if they had been for sale.

After a sumptuous French dinner (I would have preferred Persian cuisine), we drank coffee and conversed. The room had a *kursi* for those who wanted extra warmth. A *kursi* is a brazier with live coals around, and people sit or recline with blankets raised over the brazier and themselves from foot to shoulders. Malek's daughter availed herself of the *kursi,* and since the room was not chilly, I asked if she felt cold. "Not really," she explained, "but I live in a modern apartment with central heating. When I visit Father, I like to be reminded of the good old days."

After a while, Malek took me aside and told me that he had always wanted a son with whom to share the joy of studying his library of manuscripts. But, alas, Khoda (God) had granted him only daughters, and they had married businessmen with no cultural interests. He invited me to remain with him after the war so that we could study his manuscripts and publish those that were of special interest to me. Had there not been an academic position waiting for me in America, I would have stayed with Malek. Instead, I thanked him for his touching and attractive offer and explained that I had accepted a professorship in my native land and was thus not free to remain with him.

Malek was a true gentleman of the old school from the eastern province of Khorasan. Every Now Ruz (New Year's Day, around March 20–21) he would charter a plane and send it filled with roses to his female friends and relatives in his native province. At the end of his life, he bequeathed his collection to the Iranian nation, along with funds for constructing a fitting building to house it and an endowment for maintaining it properly.

Unlike my prior contacts in the Arab world, where I had met mostly illiterate peasants, seminomads, and nomads, the people I met in Iran were primarily from the upper crust: princes (mainly of the wealthy, though ousted, Qajar Dynasty, because members of the new Pahlavi Dynasty were few in number), generals, land owners, and professionals such as physicians, lawyers, and engineers—all members of the "four hundred families" who controlled and ruled the country. The clergy had no noticeable influence; rather, the mullahs were the subject of comic stories about a whimsical medieval priest named Mullah Nasru-d-Din. Such tales were much loved by the Iranians I knew, but they did not inspire reverence for the clergy. I would like to tell dozens of tales about Mullah Nasru-d-Din but shall limit myself to only a few.

One day the Mullah was at home with his wife when a funeral procession was passing by. The mourners, acting out the traditional signs of grief and sobbing to the corpse, cried, "How can you leave us to go to a place where there is no food, nothing to drink, nothing to keep you warm, and no one to love you?" Hearing this, Nasru-d-Din shouted to his wife, "Woman! Shut the windows and bolt the doors! The deceased is heading this way!"

On another occasion Nasru-d-Din knew that his neighbor wanted to borrow a certain donkey, but Nasru-d-Din did not want to lend it to him. So he locked the donkey inside his house and sat outside on the steps. When the neighbor came and asked to borrow the donkey, Nasru-d-Din replied, "I'm sorry to inform you that I have already lent him to someone else." At that moment, the donkey began to bray. The offended neighbor upbraided the Mullah and asked, "What kind of Muslim priest are you? You have lied to me!" Nasru-d-Din replied, "What kind of Muslim are you? I am a mullah, with a long white beard, and I know the Qur'an. Are you going to believe me or that donkey?"

Finally, in Nasru-d-Din's village, the bakery produced bread only once a week. The Mullah arrived late at the bakery one morning; a long line of villagers waiting to buy bread had already formed. To get to the head of the line, the Mullah cried to the crowd, "You fools! You stand in line to spend your hard-earned money on bread, when around the corner they are offering delicious chelo kebab for free!" The crowd instantly left Nasru-d-Din in a cloud of dust. Then the stunned Mullah, after regaining his equilibrium a moment later, dashed after the stampeding crowd, exclaiming, "Who knows? Maybe they are giving it away!"

As I stated earlier, the Iranians I knew found such stories comical, but they do not tell the entire story. When the Ayatollah Khomeini assumed power in Iran, I thought the fundamentalist regime would not last a year. My incorrect evaluation stemmed from the fact that my acquaintance with the Iranian people was virtually limited to a small fraction of the upper 1 percent. I did not realize what a hold the mullahs had on the population as a whole. To understand any country realistically, one needs a well-rounded knowledge of its population. Several lessons I learned in Middle Eastern affairs over the years illustrate what I mean.

In 1931, an educated Iraqi in Mosul told me, "You seem to want to understand the political realities of the Middle East. It is simple: without terror (*ḫôf*) there is no security. There are two kind of terror: the fear (*ḫôf*) of Allah and the fear (*ḫôf*) of the government. We must have one or the other. Without them, there is chaos, and mortal danger lurks everywhere." It is difficult to translate his wise words into clear English, but one can see that the "fear of Allah" goes hand in hand with religious tyranny, the "fear of the government" with secular tyranny. Accordingly, in the Middle East, without some sort of tyranny, chaos reigns. When we read in our press that we must support some Iranian leader who will bring democracy (American style) to his country, it is sheer nonsense.

In May 1993, I was in a Muslim home in East Jerusalem. Both Arab men in the room had attended Ivy League schools, and each held a Ph.D. One of them was fervently pro-Israel; the other, bitterly anti-Israel. Among many of my Jewish Israeli friends were those so passionately opposed to Prime Minister Rabin that I feared chaos might prevail, if ever he were assassinated by the Likud opposition. When I expressed this worry to my Arab hosts, they broke into peals of laughter. I asked them what was so funny, and they replied, "Don't you know that Israel is the only country in the Middle East where political assassination is not institutionalized? In Israel, if the prime minister loses his majority in the Kenesset, the president asks another political leader to try to form a viable cabinet. But the opposition does not assassinate anyone. In other Middle East countries, a bullet takes the place of parliamentary procedures and the ballot box, but not here."

It is true that the United States maintains agencies such as the CIA that commit violent acts. Our government has in the past tried to shroud such acts in secrecy, but our public is embarrassed and even ashamed to learn about them. In the Near East, however, terrorist governments and fanatical parties gleefully take credit for heinous terrorist atrocities. There is a difference between being ashamed of evil, on the one hand, and being proud of it, on the other. Sadly, the assassination of Rabin in 1995 by a Jewish fanatic showed that I, in my ignorance of what these better-informed Arab friends "knew," had been prophetically right.

My years in the Near East taught me many lessons, some good and some bad, but they also allowed me to meet many fascinating people. Among the prominent Iranians I met while I was stationed in Tehran was a man known by the family title Malek-esh-Shoʿara ("King of Poets"). This individual, whose actual family name was Bahar, knew only two languages, Persian and Arabic, but he wrote encyclopedic books requiring a vast amount of assorted information. It was remarkable that he knew as much as he did, since he did not have access to French, German, English, and other European books and periodicals.

I encountered Malek-esh-Shoʿara as a result of my association with Mohammad Movaqqar, the wealthy owner of the newspaper *Mehr-e-Iran* ("Love of Iran"). One day Movaqqar invited me to his home, where he had a collection of antiquities in showcases tastefully adorning his parlor. In one of them I saw two Aramaic magic bowls, which I told him I could translate and would like to publish. Suspecting a scam, he replied that he would not pay me for doing so. I assured him that as a U.S. Army officer, I did not feel free to accept lucrative employment of any kind while I was on active duty.

Agha-ye- ("Mr.") Movaqqar remained unconvinced. Most Iranians regarded the American forces as competent barbarians who could win a war but who lacked any cultural accomplishments, such as knowledge of Aramaic. Agha-ye-Movaqqar obviously held this view, so he asked me, "Would you be willing to submit to an Aramaic examination by our great scholar, Malek-esh-Shoʿara?" "With pleasure," I replied.

The examination, which the Iranian press corps was invited to witness, was set for noon the next day in Agha-ye-Movaqqar's parlor. At noon everyone except the distinguished King of Poets was there drinking tea. Movaqqar sat next to me and quietly admitted, "Our great King of Poets has an unfortunate Iranian habit: opium. He smokes it every morning but usually recovers from the stupor in time to make noon appointments. He is late today, but his servants just phoned to assure me he will be here in good shape by 1:00 P.M." As promised, several minutes before 1:00, in walked the King of Poets, sharp as a tack.

Although my examiner did not know Aramaic, he had learned, from my old mentor Ernst Herzfeld, the Arameograms known as *huzvaresh*. In Pahlavi (i.e., Middle Persian) there are quite a few Aramaic words meant to be pronounced in Persian. So he asked me to tell how *lahma* was to be pronounced. I responded with *nan* (which means "bread"), and, to the amazement of the audience of journalists, the King of Poets exclaimed: "bah, bah, bah!" ("good, good, good!"). Then he asked me how *huzvaresh bisra* is to be pronounced. I replied with *gusht* ("meat"), to which he again exclaimed, "bah, bah, bah!" Next he asked about *Malkin-Malka,* which I rendered in Persian as *Shahin-Shah* ("King of kings"). After I correctly translated several more Arameograms, the King of Poets proclaimed me a great Aramaic scholar, which the press relayed to the public the next day.

Years later I published both of Agha-ye-Movaqqar's magic bowls in *Orientalia*. They appeared shortly before a visit of his to Princeton, where I lived after the war, so I was able to give him reprints in person. In the article I thanked him as a prominent publisher and a distinguished collector of antiquities, which, of course, "made his day" at Princeton. But this was not the first publication of these bowls. Soon after I had passed the examination, my introduction to, translation of, and commentary on one of the bowls was printed in Persian in *Mehr-e-Iran*. This made of me a celebrity in Tehran, much to the delight of my Iranian friends and to the amazement of the general reading public, who learned for the first time that a PGC officer was not necessarily an uncultivated barbarian.

After the war, Malek-esh-Shoʿara became Iran's minister of education, and he was honored as a distinguished citizen for the rest of his life. In America, I doubt that a known opium addict could assume a respected role in the life of the nation, but Iran is not America. There may well be no absolute, international standards of personal life, but dependable people with no identity crisis will make the most of themselves by practicing the virtues of their own people and limiting themselves to the vices of their own people. An upstanding Saudi may have four wives at one time but may drink no liquor. On the other hand, a solid American is permitted to enjoy liquor in moderation but must shun polygamy.

In reality, standards and expectations vary, as I learned at a small but interesting dinner party. One of the guests was the head of a religious political party. He bore the impressive title of Temeddunu-l-Mulk ("The Culture of the Realm"). He drank wine copiously and with gusto. However, another guest, an Afghan Army major, impressed me with his gentlemanliness and unobtrusive Muslim piety. Without showing disapproval of Temeddunu-l-Mulk's flouting of Islamic rules, he merely acted as a follower of the Prophet should. My curiosity piqued by the disparity between the two, I asked Temeddunu-l-Mulk how he reconciled enjoyment of forbidden alcohol with his public advocacy of Islamic piety. He replied, "People need either religion or education. My ignorant followers need religion, whereas I am educated." At the time, I thought this was inexcusable hypocrisy. Now that I have seen more of the world, I am not so judgmental. In that culture, the answer made sense, though I must admit that I still respect the Afghan major more than Mr. "Culture of the Realm."

Iranian culture was not the only one that I learned during the war years. I also discovered a great deal about the military culture, of which I was a part. Once André Kostelanetz and his wife Lilly Pons visited the PGC and regaled us and the dignitaries of Tehran with a concert on a Saturday evening. That afternoon, prior to the concert, I made the mistake of going to my office. On weekends a normal soldier takes off to have fun and stays out of his superiors' reach. A general found me at my desk and said, "Lieutenant, I have discovered an embarrassing breach of protocol. We have prepared only an English program for tonight's concert. You must prepare a Persian translation of the program immediately."

When I protested that I had never even composed a program in English and that I had no notion of Persian musical terminology, he replied bluntly: "I have given you a direct order, which you will obey." So I sat down at my Arabic-Persian typewriter and began to prepare a stencil of the program in Persian. The technical musical terminology I took from the only detailed Persian dictionary at my disposal. It had been published about half a century earlier, and many changes had taken place in the meantime, especially under the tremendous impact of Western music. But I did the best I could, then found several enlisted men to mimeograph enough copies for our expected guests. Not surprisingly, that night at the concert I noted amused smiles on the faces of the Shahin-Shah, the Empress, his Imperial Majesty's ministers, and the intellectual elite of Iran.

I had at last learned the working of the military mind, which operates by fiat. Is this not the way that God created the world when he said, "Let there be light" and "there was light"? Military dictatorships are usually inefficient because the minister of agriculture is a general who usually knows nothing about farming, the minister of commerce is likewise a general who usually knows nothing about business and trade, and so on. Military dictatorships rule by fiat, which produces results like my Persian program.

My military assignments took me all through western Iran, from steaming hellholes such as Andimeshk to the great centers of Iranian culture, such as Shiraz, Isfahan, and Hamadan. Shiraz is the capital of the province of Fars, or Persia. The historical importance of Fars can be seen in several ways. First, in Iran today only the people of Fars are called Farsi, which means "Persian." Moreover, the language of Iran is Persian because it was the speech of Fars.

Hamadan, on the other hand, is the site of the capital of ancient Media. Cyrus the Great, a Persian emperor, united the Medes and Persians to form the nucleus of the Achaemenid Empire, which eventually constituted 127 provinces and ruled the habitable world from India to Ethiopia (Esth 1:1). He also sent the Hebrews who had been exiled by the Babylonians back home to rebuild Jerusalem and the temple. For this Cyrus was called "his anointed" ("his messiah") in Isa 45:1. My father, an ardent Zionist, named me for Cyrus the Great and Theodore Herzl.

Fars includes the ruins of Persepolis, the capital of the Achaemenid Empire. This grand city was built primarily by Darius I and Xerxes I, but their followers also constructed additions. Cyrus's earlier capital, Pasargade, is also in Fars, and near it is the well-preserved tomb of Cyrus. Among my pilgrimages to the old Persian capital built by the man after whom I am named was one that I made on the Persian Now Ruz (New Year's Day). There I met another pilgrim, a Zardushti (Zoroastrian). Our meeting was cordial, for we were both honoring the memory of the same great king.

Isfahan, the showplace of Islamic Iran, is filled with the well-preserved glories of the Sefavid Dynasty, whose most noteworthy ruler, Shah Abbas I the Great, reigned from 1588 to 1629. Iranians still say, "Isfahan nisf-e-Jahan" ("Isfahan is half the world"). As in most countries, the people of Iran's various cities have different dispositions. The Isfahanis have the reputation of being stingy. The Shirazis, on the other hand, are said to be carefree, enjoying wine, gambling, sex, and other joys without counting the cost. After the war, I made two trips to Mashhad, the holiest of the Iranian pilgrimage cities, where the Imam Reza is buried. There, among the pilgrims, I noted a number of Shirazi penitents. After offering their prayers and other devotions to wipe away their sins, they would return to Shiraz with cleansed souls and begin a new round of sinful pleasures. Religion need not be austere; it can gladden what otherwise might be a vale of toil and tears.

I would much like to relate at further length my experiences in Iran, but doing so might endanger the completion of this book. So without more ado, I will get on with the rest of my life's story.

The Allied victory in Europe effectively ended the mission of the PGC, for the Russians no longer needed the lend-lease supplies to fight the already vanquished Germans on the eastern front. So in June 1945, I boarded a transport plane filled with troops and flew to Italy, where I was billeted in a camp near Pozzuoli (ancient Petuoli) at the north end of the Bay of Naples. Much to my delight, there was such a shortage of transport planes and ships that I was able to enjoy an entire month of sightseeing in the Naples area, with no duties to perform.

Several times a week, I went to the San Carlo Opera. The typical audience was far from socially elite, but they had a thorough knowledge of

Italian opera. During the intermissions, they would discuss and compare previous performances, thus revealing a detailed and critical familiarity with the subject. On the streets people often sang, and while some of the voices were good, many were quite bad. When everyone is a performing artist, the average product is bound to be mediocre, and much of it downright inferior.

Naples had suffered severe bombing, especially along the waterfront. One parish and its church, however, had escaped the damage. Its people were telling members of other parishes things such as, "Didn't we tell you that our Madonna was the real one?" Simple faith is hardly ecumenical.

The Doric Greek temples at Pestum, south of Naples, are not as graceful as the Parthenon in Athens, but they are a bit older and better preserved. The present name of the site, Pesto, is a worn-down form of Poseidonium. Indeed, *Naples* is the Greek term for "New City" (*Nea + polis*). Moreover, Southern Italy was called *Magna Graecia,* from which we, via Roman Europe, designate the Hellenic world as *Greece.* The Greeks, however, do not call themselves Greek nor their country Greece, except for foreign consumption.

Once I was lucky enough to get a three-day holiday at an "R and R" (recreation and recuperation) center that had been set up on the island of Capri in the Bay of Naples. The American troops there (fine, largely young and riotous "flak-happy" aviators with whom I spent little time) were billeted at an attractive hotel, the Quisisana. I spent most of my time familiarizing myself with the island, especially the imperial palace from which Tiberius ruled the great Roman Empire. I had visited the actual palace during an earlier visit in the 1930s, but it was out of bounds, on account of archaeological operations, in 1945.

Vesuvius belched forth its menacing smoke over the ruins of Herculaneum and Pompeii. But on the slopes of Vesuvius, peasants live and cultivate the soil. People often cling to their home even though it marks the site of a catastrophe waiting to happen again.

In retrospect, all my travels and experiences have contributed to my gradual development into a student who views the habitable world as a single ecumene. My month in Italy en route from Iran to the United States in 1945 played a key role in the process.

The voyage from Italy to the States was peaceful. This time we did not need to make sure that the enlisted men did not escape prior to embarkation. As I have already observed, all we needed to do was to remind them that if they missed the boat they might have to wait a long time before another ship was available to take them home.

I was happy to see my parents and siblings. Moreover, while I was in Iran, a full professorship in Assyriology had been offered to me at Dropsie College, then a Ph.D. granting institution with no undergraduate program.

I would begin work as soon as I was separated from the Army. Meanwhile, Japan was forced to surrender and the Second World War was over. A number of our generals, who did not want to lose their comfortable positions, retained their troops in hopes of prolonging their active service by commanding the armies occupying the Far East, including Japan.

Because I was in the PGC, which was a transportation command, after ninety days home leave with pay, I was assigned to Camp Plauchee in the swamps near New Orleans, training with transportation officers for service in Japan. My duties included packing crates in the steaming swamps, where every swarm of insects was followed in several days by another of a different species. Working under these conditions, I broke out with prickly heat. The military had enacted a new rule specifying that military personnel could be separated from the service only by the accumulation of points. My points made it uncertain as to when I could get out and return to my academic career.

My fellow officers and I got along well with each other, but since they were career stevedores, sailors, railroad men, and truckers, they realized that their way of life was significantly different from mine. This came out rather strikingly on one occasion. Since we hardly enjoyed our training in the swampy camp, we went out in the evenings to dine in New Orleans. One of the stevedore officers told me that he had discovered a superb bar and steak restaurant in town. When I asked if I might join him that evening, he hastened to explain why I would not fit in with him and his fellow stevedores, who would go to the bar and pick a fight with merchant mariners regarding who were the better stevedores. Then, after beating up the merchant mariners and thereby working up a hearty appetite, my fellow officers would sit down to a delicious steak dinner. My buddy concluded with the sound observation that I would not really like the evening's program.

Through the help of friends in the Historical Section in Washington, I managed to get transferred to it until I got out on points by February 1946. The idea of writing the history of World War II was not only to record the facts for posterity and to take pride in our victories but also to expose our mistakes so that they would not be repeated in the future. I had already learned that commanding generals saw to it that their official histories were completely laudatory and not in any way critical. This was a valuable lesson for a scholar because it was forever thus. When we read the annals and "histories" of the past, we must not accept them at face value. They are all too often tendentious and propagandistic.

As I was mustered out of the military, I was asked if I would remain a reservist. Since I had been raised with the ideal of being a citizen-soldier, I indicated that it was my intention to remain in the ready reserves, at which point a promotion to captain was automatically conferred upon me.

During my years of active service, I had been given such lukewarm efficiency reports by my immediate superiors that I never rose above the rank of first lieutenant. I think that I deserved much better treatment for the level of service that I rendered, such as establishing America's first agency to cryptanalyze Arabic, Turkish, and Persian codes and ciphers, and successfully solving every system in record time.

After World War II, the United States established an independent Air Force, equal with the Army and Navy. The overall educational level of the Air Force was so far below that of the other two branches that the Air Force embarked on a vigorous campaign to secure highly educated officers to supplement its heroic but flak-happy and undereducated military personnel. The Air Force offered the rank of lieutenant colonel to desirable candidates with at least nineteen years of post-Ph.D., useful professional experience. I therefore switched from the Army to the Air Force Reserve, gaining a double promotion without ever occupying the rank of major.

Subsequently, on my annual summer tours of active duty, as the ranking Air Force intelligence officer on Middle East affairs, I prepared reports that the regular career Air Force officers greatly appreciated. This time there was no jealousy, for as a reservist I was not in competition for their jobs. My efficiency reports soon won for me a promotion to full colonel.

6.
TENURE AT LAST!

Dropsie

Dropsie College had already played a key role in my development as a scholar. As I have already observed, Max Margolis, who taught there from 1909 until 1932, taught me the ins and outs of Semitic linguistics, which enabled me to compose my *Ugaritic Grammar*. Now Dropsie, however, offered me the opportunity to teach hard-working students in a serious program.[26] Most of the students came from conservative Protestant backgrounds. The first to graduate was G. Douglas Young; the second, William Sanford LaSor.[27] Both were students of outstanding ability. They were, nevertheless, branded as fundamentalists by liberal Christian scholars of the Old Testament.

There are, in my opinion, two kinds of fundamentalists. The majority can be described as "born educated." Believing that they already know everything, they think that it is impossible for anyone to teach them anything. But there is a minority who start with the premise that, although the Truth is in the Bible, it is not always found in the English translations. If one wants to know the *verbum domini*, one has to seek it in the Hebrew OT and Greek NT. Learning those two languages is an intellectual achievement. Moreover, if the teachers they respect claim that to understand the biblical world, they must also learn the sources of that world, sources recorded in Akkadian cuneiform and Egyptian hieroglyphs, they strive their utmost to do it.

---

[26] The Dropsie College for Hebrew and Cognate Learning was organized in 1907 in Philadelphia and chartered in 1909. The school was funded by the will of Moses Dropsie (1821–1905). The first president of Dropsie was Cyrus Adler (1863–1940).

[27] George Douglas Young (1910–1980) served as Dean of Trinity Evangelical Divinity School from 1958 until 1978. He founded the American Institute of Holy Land Studies in Jerusalem and, having moved to Jerusalem, was director at the time of his death.

LaSor, who had also studied at Princeton, received the Ph.D. at Dropsie in 1949. He taught Old Testament at Fuller Theological Seminary from 1949 to 1980. His many and varied published works centered on the Dead Sea Scrolls.

The latter type came to study with me because I approach Scripture, as well as all texts, with the aim of first understanding the text as it is. I am not interested in altering a text in order to prove any theological or other preconceived idea. They trusted my integrity and knew that I respected their sacred text. In the process, they ripened into broad-minded scholars with complete contempt for the "born educated." Finally, their own colleges and seminaries pursued my students for the academic prestige such faculty members would bring.

One of my early graduates was William Rossell, who went on to be appointed to the Old Testament chair at Central Baptist Seminary in Kansas City, Kansas. He served there successfully for several years, then left to accept a professorship at the large and influential Southwestern Baptist Seminary in Fort Worth, Texas. At that point the president of Central Baptist phoned me to say he wanted another one of my students to take Rossell's place. So I recommended Fred Young, who became Professor of Old Testament and later also Dean of Central Baptist.

Some years later I received a similar indication of the dent I was making in conservative Protestant biblical studies. I had been asked to speak as the annual guest lecturer at Fuller Theological Seminary. In his introduction, the president observed that over twenty of the leading conservative Protestant Old Testament professors in America were my students. He concluded by stating, "I present to you Dr. Gordon, who, though not Christian, is through his students a leading figure in conservative Christian Old Testament studies."

The four war years (1941–1945) that kept me away from academic institutions had several effects on my scholarship and my teaching. For example, the accepted way to analyze the Pentateuch was to divide it into four hypothetical sources: J, E, D, and P. One of the presumed characteristics of P (the Priestly Code, supposedly from the time of the Second Temple, ca. fifth century B.C.E.) was a preoccupation with details such as the measurements of Noah's ark. However, while at Dropsie I reread the description of Utnapishtim's ark in the Gilgamesh Epic and observed a similar concern with detailed specifications. If this feature obliged us to attribute the Genesis account to P of the fifth century, it must, I reasoned, do the same for the Babylonian account, which is absurd. I also found other absurdities in the so-called higher criticism of the Establishment. If *Yahweh-Elohim* owed its origin to the combination of God's name in J (*Jehovah* is the mistaken reading of *Yahweh*) with his name in E (*Elohim*), then every Egyptian inscription mentioning the god Amon-Re must have derived the name from an A-document combined with an R-document. One might also argue the same for Ugaritic documents, which abound with divine names composed of two elements. I documented every step carefully and, in the process, alienated many liberal Christian and Jewish colleagues, who accused me of playing into the hands of the Protestant fundamentalists. I did not yet fully realize that in any establishment, changes in detail may be tolerated but not the rejection of the system as a whole.[28]

The Dropsie years were productive. I published much and taught courses on Assyriology, Egyptology, Hebrew linguistics, and other Near Eastern subjects such as Aramaic magic bowls. Still, I was not happy with the administration. Dropsie's president, Abraham A. Neuman, was not only dictatorial, but he committed the blunder of introducing inappropriate departments, such as Education and Near Eastern Politics, that gradually stripped the school of its essential character and contributed to its downfall. However, I was able to learn, teach, and publish so much during my decade at Dropsie that I can only evaluate my time there as a (*faute de mieux*) great opportunity of which I took full advantage by fulfilling my mission to the best of my ability.

Neuman underpaid his faculty and offered them no retirement plan. Instead, most professors taught and collected their full salary until they expired. By remaining as a captain in the Army Reserve, I supplemented my income with the salary that I received for completing temporary active duty during summer vacations. More important, after finishing twenty years of combined active and reserve service, I would earn retired pay for life, starting on my sixtieth birthday. At this time I also succeeded in securing paid lectures through a lecture agency. As I increased my outside income, I decreased my sense of enslavement to Abraham Neuman, who had explicitly told me that, as a professor, I was destined to a life of poverty and that the sooner I accepted that fact the better it would be for all concerned. I knew that Neuman was wrong.

I do not like to criticize anyone while passing over his virtues in silence. So, in fairness to Neuman, I recall an incident that reflects a more commendable side of his presidency. Seven of my doctoral students felt a need for a course in Sumerian. When I asked Neuman to approve my offering Sumerian in the following year, he asked, "Will there be any students to take such a course?" I assured him that there were already seven ready to sign up, to which he responded, "That's wonderful! I would approve such a course even if there were only two qualified students, and perhaps even for one."

A bit of background on Dropsie will help explain Neuman's attitude at a time when many universities were so bent on cost-accounting that a small enrollment justified canceling a course no matter how serious the subject might be. The first president of Dropsie was Cyrus Adler, who was among the earliest Ph.D.'s trained at Johns Hopkins University, America's

---

[28] See "Higher Critics and Forbidden Fruit," *ChrTod* 4 (Nov. 23, 1959): 3–6.

first and then foremost graduate school.[29] Adler believed in the ideals of Hopkins and applied them to Dropsie. Neuman, in turn, idolized Adler and succeeded him as president. Thus, Neuman's enthusiastic support of my Sumerian course was ultimately a product of the standards set by Johns Hopkins University.

Dropsie was located in Northeast Philadelphia, but I chose to live in Princeton, New Jersey, during the years that I taught there (1946–1956). The drive from home to Dropsie was less than an hour, door to door, and Princeton had a fine library, including the endowed David Patton Collection of books in my field. At that time Philip K. Hitti stressed Arabic and did less than justice to Assyriology, Egyptology, and, indeed, the entire pre-Islamic Near East. This meant that I had, in effect, the Patton Collection for my own use. I also enjoyed the intellectual stimulation of my friends at the Institute for Advanced Study and at Princeton Theological Seminary. Henry S. Gehman, an Old Testament specialist, was a close friend of mine, and I also knew Bruce Metzger.[30]

At that time Princeton University was strong in the sciences but weak in the humanities. One humanist, however, Professor Giuliano Bonfante, brightened my years in Princeton. He was a general linguist specializing in comparative Romance linguistics. I owe a great deal to Bonfante, for he enabled me to break out of the confines of nineteenth-century German linguistics (which, with its emphasis on phonetic law, still offers an excellent foundation) and to apply the results of other schools of linguistics, such as the geographical linguistics of Matteo Giulio Bartoli (1873–1946).

In addition to imparting to me intellectual stimulation, Bonfante's wit and foibles provided me endless amusement. Like a number of upper-class North Italian intellectuals, Giuliano took a robust pleasure in sin without the restraints advocated by his Catholic heritage. Once he, another Princeton scholar, and I planned to attend conferences in Chicago during

---

[29] Cyrus Adler (1863–1940) was born in Van Buren, Arkansas. He took the A.B. (1883) and the M.A. (1886) from the University of Pennsylvania. In 1887 he received a Ph.D. in Assyriology from Johns Hopkins University. In 1888 he became involved in the Jewish Publication Society. In 1908 he was appointed president of Dropsie, then in 1915 of the Jewish Theological Seminary, serving both schools concurrently. He was very influential in Washington, D.C., and advised many U.S. presidents on Jewish affairs.

[30] Bruce Metzger (b. 1914) was born in Middleton, Pennsylvania. He received the B.A. in 1935 from Lebanon Valley College, then the Th.B. (1938), Th.M. (1939), M.A. (1940), and Ph.D. (1942) from Princeton Theological Seminary. He was a professor at Princeton Theological Seminary from 1940 to 1984. He is among America's foremost experts on the text of the New Testament. He has served as the chairman of the RSV/NRSV committee since 1975.

the academic recess between Christmas and New Year's. In those days, the railroad sold, at a bargain rate, a group round-trip ticket to any three bona fide academicians from a specific area who were attending learned society meetings held in any one city in the country. The restriction was that the three had to travel together, going and returning on the same group ticket. Giuliano and I usually sat together.

On the way back from Chicago, Giuliano informed me that he had received good news. His uncle, Michaele Rua, a priest who had died forty-five years earlier, had just been beatified and as a *beatus* was eligible for promotion to *sanctus*. I told Giuliano that I was glad for him and his family and that it was an honor for me to be a friend of a saint's nephew. But then I asked, "Why is it that an egregious sinner of your ilk takes such delight in having a saint in your family?" "You do not understand the function of saints," he explained. "It is not for their own benefit that they are beatified and sanctified, but for us sinners. Their job is to intercede and get forgiveness for us. So not only I, but my friends like you, should escalate our sinning because my sainted uncle should not be underemployed."

Near the end of our ride we had to change trains at North Philadelphia station to board a train that would stop at Princeton Junction, where we could change to the shuttle connecting with Princeton. It was Sunday, and the train we boarded at North Philadelphia was so crowded that we could not find seats together. Giuliano sat next to a young lady and struck up a lively conversation with her. At Trenton, I went over to Giuliano and said, "I do not like to interrupt, but in a few minutes we have to get off at Princeton Junction. If you fail to do so, the next stop is Newark." This was bad news for Giuliano, but he did what he had to do. With a heavy heart he bade farewell to the attractive young woman, and we began to make our way through the crowded train toward the exit. To make light of the situation, I said, "Dear friend, do not be so dejected. For all you know, this is the work of your sainted uncle in heaven to preserve you from the pitfall of sin." Giuliano was not amused. Red with anger, he shouted, "God damn my sainted uncle in heaven! It's his business to forgive, not prevent sin!"

Among the courses I taught at Dropsie was Egyptian. How I learned Egyptian is something of a saga. Years earlier, Sam Kramer and I had been the only students to sign up for Nathaniel Reich's course in the Egyptian language. His method involved translating the German text of Röder's *Aegyptische Grammatik* into English. After the second lesson Professor Reich pointed an accusing finger at Sam and me and said, "Everything you have learned in my class is mine. Don't publish it!" That was enough for Sam and me, and we never returned for the third lesson.

Some years later, William Albright offered a course on Egyptian. Again, two people signed up for it: Gladys Davidson and I. But then Albright ordered me to withdraw, leaving him with a class of one. When I asked him why he had expelled me, he explained, "You already know too many languages." He did not want me to become a rival Semitist who also knew Egyptian.

When I was called to Dropsie as Professor of Assyriology, I was told, at the eleventh hour, that my full title was "Professor of Assyriology and Egyptology." This, of course, created a bit of a problem, since I had never actually completed a course in Egyptian. However, in my Army assignment I had become a friend of William Edgerton, in civilian life a professor of Egyptology at the Oriental Institute of the University of Chicago. So I asked him what I should do to get started. He advised me to work through Gardiner's *Egyptian Grammar* as I read the Egyptian Romance of Sinuhe in hieroglyphs. So that was the course I offered at Dropsie when I began teaching there in February 1946. When I was hired, I did not reveal that I could not teach Egyptian; rather, I learned it.

I remained at Dropsie until June 1956, and during ten plus years there, I read a different text with my students each semester. I alternated hieroglyphic Egyptian with Coptic and even assigned a Ph.D. dissertation to Dwight Young on Shenoute: the most classical of the Coptic Fathers. Thereafter I turned my attention to Late Egyptian, which fits linguistically between Middle Egyptian and Coptic. By 1956 I was known as one of the few American Egyptologists outside of the Oriental Institute and the University of Michigan Coptologist, William Worrell.

Brandeis University

Escape from bondage came after I read of the death of Ludwig Lewisohn in 1955, who was then on the faculty of Brandeis University. I was at that time working on the interrelation of preprophetic Hebrew and preclassical Greek literatures. I thought that Brandeis might consider me as Lewisohn's successor in comparative literature. I did not approach President Sachar of Brandeis University directly but rather worked through my influential friend, Maurice Jacobs, the owner and editor of the Jewish Publication Society. Jacobs wrote to Sachar about my availability, and I soon received an invitation to deliver a lecture at Brandeis, which I knew was for the purpose of looking me over for a faculty position there. What I did not know was that Sachar welcomed the prospect of having me join the faculty.

As it turned out, however, Sachar was not considering me for Lewisohn's post. In fact, Sachar needed me to replace his able Semitist, Wolf Leslau, whom he was firing for saying something critical about Brandeis University to acquaintances at Harvard. Sachar could be vindictive and ruthless, and he had a network of spies who reported indiscretions such as Leslau's remarks.

At any rate, I left Dropsie at the end of the 1955–1956 academic year to begin the next phase of my career. Seven doctoral candidates followed me to Brandeis, thereby launching the first real graduate department in any of the humanities at Brandeis.

Tenure at Last!

The topic of my earlier lecture had been the Dead Sea Scrolls. So after I joined the faculty, Brandeis, which expended a great deal of energy on public relations, billed me as a great authority on the Scrolls. Now, over forty years later, I am still occasionally invited by "old friends of Brandeis" to speak on the Scrolls, although my research and publications have long been in other fields. My primary interest in the Scrolls did not center on the Old Testament books they contained, but on the hitherto unknown books, such as *The Rule of the Community* (*The Manual of Discipline*), on which I did publish. At times I am still introduced as "the foremost authority on the Dead Sea Scrolls," which always makes me uncomfortable. I like to receive credit for my real accomplishments but not for honors I have not earned. Public relations is, unfortunately, often more durable than factual truth.

I started at Brandeis as a professor in the Department of Near Eastern and Judaic Studies, but that did not last for long. Bringing along my veteran doctoral students and experiencing good success in the classroom created jealousy among some of my colleagues. Eventually, the most vicious of my associates resorted to such shamelessly "dirty tricks"[31] that I told President Sachar it would be best for the university if my area were detached from Near Eastern and Judaic Studies and set up as the Department of Mediterranean Studies. This would not only solve the personal issue but also enable the study of Hebrew, Greek, and Latin civilizations to be integrated with the cuneiform world and Egypt. My idea appealed to Sachar, who immediately implemented my request. Thus began the most dynamic period of my teaching career.

Desirable Ph.D. candidates to the Department of Mediterranean Studies came with a facility for languages, especially Hebrew, Latin, and Greek. They understood the necessity to sight-read French and German for their secondary sources. If they could not make the grade, however, they would, after two years, receive a terminal M.A. and not be allowed to continue in the department. Gifted students, on the other hand, were exposed

---

[31] The worst of them was a knowledgeable but uncreative Judaic specialist. He lacked character but posed as a saint, which fooled many, especially good women who were looking for a man who exemplified virtue. I was chairman of the department and he visited me "to see with what sort of person he had to deal." I was then working on the decipherment of Minoan. During the winter break in December-January (1957–1958), I went to Crete to study the Minoan material there. While I was gone he summoned my students and told them they must abandon me and become his students. They explained that they could not do this because they had been studying with me for years and had followed me to Brandeis from Philadelphia. When I returned, the students told me what had happened, and, soon afterwards, the rascal came to apologize. I told him that I accepted his apology but reminded him that although we can regret our misdeeds, we cannot undo them.

to other Semitic languages, especially Akkadian, as well as Egyptian. In addition to their courses, they had to pass general oral and written examinations, as well as examinations on outside readings in history. I encouraged students to complete the entire Ph.D. course of study in no more than four years; in three, if possible. As a result, my students were easily placed because they could take jobs in many subjects: Bible, ancient (even modern) Near East, archaeology, history, and the like.

More important than the results of their general exams and their dissertation, however, was whether or not I was confident that they could succeed in positions far from the great academic centers, such as New York City or Boston. When I felt that they could thrive in places such as North Dakota or, God forbid, Alaska, they were ready to be awarded a Ph.D.

I was privileged to teach a number of excellent students at Brandeis. Martha Morrison, for example, gained mastery of the Nuzi tablets while an undergraduate at Wellesley College, then came for her doctorate at Brandeis. At that time, I held some mistaken notions about women's academic interests and abilities. I thought that women were proficient in art and archaeology but inept at linguistic science. Martha was thrown together with the other doctoral candidates into my Hebrew seminar, which included several rabbis.

At first I felt sorry for Martha, but I was pleasantly surprised when, after several weeks, she was at the head of the class, all of the men trailing far behind. They had come with a routine training in Hebrew, but she had come with an open mind and quickly benefited from the formulaic principles according to which Hebrew operates. Moreover, Martha had a natural facility for languages, and, with the help of methods I taught her for learning to read a text at sight, she rose to the top of the class at sight-reading and translating. Martha's publication record in Nuzi studies and Hurrian civilization is impressive. In addition, she received the award for being the finest teacher at Brandeis. But even beyond that, she cured me of my misapprehensions about women students, thus preparing me for the years ahead, especially at New York University, when most of my doctoral students were women.

Another student, David Owen, became an outstanding Sumerologist and the professor of Near East history and archaeology at Cornell University. When he retires, his endowed chair will bear his name. Owen keeps current with all the recent discoveries in the Near East, as his impressive publication record attests. He is, in reality, a one-person center of ancient Near Eastern studies.

The success of Jack Sasson, who taught at the University of North Carolina for over thirty years, can be best measured by his four-volume opus, *Civilizations of the Ancient Near East*. The work is the fulfillment of his original idea, and he is its editor-in-chief. Now, on his retirement from North Carolina, he is moving on to Vanderbilt University as The Mary Jane Werthan professor of Judaic and Biblical Studies.

Tenure at Last!

Harry Hoffner's ability was obvious to me from the start. Yale University was the center of Hittite Studies in the United States when he was a student. Sturtevant had died, and Götze was nearing retirement. So I groomed Hoffner for a post at Yale, advising him to write his Ph.D. dissertation on a Hittite topic. On graduation, he received a position at Yale, but things went awry. After losing his post at Yale, he was hired by the Oriental Institute of the University of Chicago, where he now serves as the editor of the *Chicago Hittite Dictionary,* a project that he conceived and began while a student at Brandeis. Hoffner is undeniably America's foremost Hittitologist, on his way to becoming the foremost in the world.

If I were to list and to describe the achievements of the approximately sixty Ph.D. students I mentored at Brandeis, it would more than exceed the space limits of this autobiography. Let me just say that I am proud of them all.

Once I had two Coptic students at the same time in my graduate classes. One was a priest and quite stupid. In a class on Aramaic magic bowls, I was explaining the difference between an incubus, who impregnates women by impersonating their husbands, and a succuba, who becomes pregnant by impersonating a wife. In amazement, the priest exclaimed, "And you believe such things, Professor?!" He simply could not understand that a graduate course in philology is not like a course in a theological school, which aims at inculcating articles of faith.

On the other hand, the other Coptic student, Fawzi Fahim Gadalla, was quite bright. He had originally wanted to be an Arabist and so became a disciple of the Egyptian Muslim scholar, Taha Husain. An honest man, Taha Husain advised Fawzi that a Copt would never be allowed to teach Arabic in the hopelessly bigoted land of Egypt, not even in the first grade of children's schools. The reason for this is that Arabic, unlike other languages, is held to be created by Allah and thus sacred, not to be desecrated by unbelievers. Jolted, Fawzi switched his career path to Egyptology, including Coptic.

I accepted Fawzi as a doctoral candidate and showed a real interest in him. This infuriated the stupid priest, who had accused me of being anti-Coptic. When he was informed that Fawzi was also Coptic, his wrath shifted to Fawzi. The priest turned to a Coptic bishop studying Religious Education at Princeton Theological Seminary. It did not take the bishop long to size up the situation. He called on me and said, "You don't have to worry about Fawzi. He is gifted and will find his way to succeed. Instead, you should be a good shepherd and worry about the priest, who is a lost sheep and needs your guidance." I told the bishop that I respected his humane concern but that we were in very different professions. I had to train scholars, not whiten black sheep. He admitted that I was right, and we parted as friends.

When I first came to Brandeis, I had already been working on the problem of Minoan Linear A. Michael Ventris had deciphered the Cretan language called Linear B as Greek and recognized that Linear A was not Greek. In a discussion of Mycenaean vessel names, which the scribe wrote both pictographically and syllabically on one tablet, he wrote,

> That the practice is inherited from Linear A is suggested by the Agia Triada tablet HT 31 (PM, iv, p.732, fig. 717), where the vessels are annotated with sign-groups corresponding to Linear B *su-pu* and *ka-ro-pa₃*, cups with *pa₃-pa₃*, *su-pa₃-ra* and *pa-ta-qe:* the difference of language is obvious.[32]

I was intrigued by words they listed that described various vessels. I knew these to be Semitic words, which is what started my study of Linear A.

Within my first year at Brandeis, I announced that I had deciphered Minoan Linear A through the efficient office of Public Affairs, headed by Manny Gilbert. Linear A, a Northwest Semitic language, is the earliest known translatable language in the Mediterranean, underlying both Homer and the Bible. Eventually my work on Minoan and Ugaritic led me to write *The Common Background of Greek and Hebrew Civilizations.* Though my work on Linear A has been called controversial, no scholar has yet offered a viable alternative. Unable to refute my work, many scholars have chosen rather to ignore, dismiss, or dogmatically deny it. In some circles it is unacceptable that something so basic to European culture should be Semitic.[33]

News of the decipherment made headlines all over the world, being featured on radio and television in this country and abroad. It established Brandeis as an internationally known, well-rounded university with a creative humanistic faculty. Previously Brandeis was highly regarded only in the sciences and in Judaica. The announcement that Mediterranean Studies had produced the decipherment of Minoan transformed Brandeis into a university with a creative graduate school, including the humanities. Applications for admission came in from the ends of the earth. The best years of my career had begun, but to sustain the momentum into the distant future I would need the continued support of the Brandeis administration (= Abram Sachar) that I had earned. But that was not to be.

The acclaim in the press far exceeded anything that I, or anyone else, ever anticipated. A leading New York newspaper chose me to be their "Man in the News." Then one day Sachar and I chanced to meet in a hallway of a university building. Forcing a smile, he stated, "This is no longer Brandeis University but Gordon University."

From that moment I should have recognized that he would squeeze every drop of publicity for his university out of me, then make my life there

---

[32] M. Ventris and J. Chadwick, *Documents in Mycenaean Greek* (Cambridge: Cambridge University Press, 1956), 228.

[33] See "Minoan Linear A," *JNES* 17 (1958):245–55.

impossible. That is how he treated "name people," whom he used for his own ends until they posed a threat to his absolute rule. Sachar was quite able, and he performed a feat unmatched in twentieth-century America: he built a research university from scratch. But his disposition was less than commendable.[34] Sachar exemplifies the fact that "evil" people can be constructive, whereas, alas, many a good person is unconstructive.[35]

Even so, the pain he caused me has not blinded me to the fact that he made possible my best years in the halls of academe. For example, during my Brandeis years I initiated a number of productive innovations, including marine archaeology and maritime civilizations. Marine archaeology is significant because a ship sunk in antiquity can offer a unit of civilization preserved intact. Several ships have, in fact, been found, notably one off Cape Gelidoniya near Bodrum. Archaeologists should always remember that every port has both land and underwater aspects. Caesarea is a good example of this.

Elisha Linder, Israel's pioneer underwater archaeologist, wanted to take his Ph.D. under my tutelage. He already had an M.A. from Columbia, where he had studied Akkadian, Ugaritic, and other kindred subjects under Isaac Mendelsohn. Linder's Hebrew, biblical and modern, was superb. Instead of approaching me directly, he asked his friend, Professor Harold Edgerton of M.I.T., an expert and pioneer in sonar and strobe photography, to request that I get Linder a fellowship. In those days, when there was no dearth of money, I had no trouble securing a fellowship to cover all his expenses, including bringing his wife and three young sons to Boston for a year.

I got to know Edgerton quite well soon after I came to Brandeis. In 1957 the announcement of my decipherment of Minoan Linear A attracted

---

[34] A recollection of that era is worth repeating. In 1948 when Brandeis was founded, Sachar had a faculty of only thirteen professors. One of them was Shlomo Marenof, who, though not an outstanding scholar, was sufficiently knowledgeable, dedicated to his work, and completely loyal to Sachar and the university. Irving Howe, who was to become a luminary in American letters, chanced to overhear Sachar saying something incredibly nice to Marenof. Howe then told me he was worried about Marenof because, when Sachar appears so well-disposed, he is about to strike a severe blow. Howe had an uncanny insight into human frailties. Later that day, Sachar summoned Marenof to his office and fired him. Marenof protested, "But I have tenure," to which Sachar replied, "That may be so, but I can make you miserable." Marenof was paid his next year's salary and told to disappear.

[35] In 1956 I was present when Sachar dedicated a new building on the campus. He rhetorically asked the guest audience, "Can I help it if the lies I've been telling are coming true?" It is a fact that many truthful people are unconstructive, while it is possible for a prevaricator to be constructive.

wide attention, and Edgerton wanted to meet me. He came from a small town in Nebraska and had married his childhood sweetheart, Esther, from the same town. His destiny required a more scientific ambiance, so he settled on M.I.T. He was an interesting teacher, and his students loved him. "Doc," for so he was called, was not a business person, but he teamed up with two students who had excellent business sense. Their company was known as "E, G and G." The E stood for Edgerton.

Doc was interested in using strobe photography and sonar for underwater archaeology. When he had become very wealthy, he decided to spend his life doing what he enjoyed, such as marine archaeology, instead of scheming how to make more money that he did not need. This reminds me (*mutatis mutandis*) of Schliemann, who wanted to excavate Troy but first made a fortune in business so as to have the wherewithal to pay for it. Edgerton was always ready to go with his equipment on marine expeditions to salvage or retrieve sunken ships, or even to explore the depths of Loch Ness in order to find out what, if anything, could be discovered about the Loch Ness Monster. Edgerton did not believe a word of the nonsense about the Monster. But if he could lay the myth to rest while he learned about the flora, fauna, and geology of Loch Ness, it was all to the good.

Before I met Doc, he had experienced a great tragedy. One of his sons had perished while working with a team trying to salvage and/or raise the *Andrea Doria*. I have been told that Doc, grief-stricken, walked around for two years like a zombie. When I first met him, he had recovered and was, at least outwardly, his old affable self. He carried around postcard-size copies of strobe pictures he had made. One was a drop of milk that had splashed on a hard red surface to produce a beautiful white corona. Another was a small caliber bullet emerging from an apple through which it had been shot.

One more observation should be made about Doc Edgerton. He never went underwater himself. He would bring the equipment, personally attend it, and, at times, direct the underwater operations from a small boat. But he always kept both feet dry. One underwater tragedy in the family was more than enough. Perhaps he had promised Esther that he would not expose himself to death under water.

On the basis of Edgerton's recommendation, I not only promised to take on Elisha Linder but also planned to devote the following year of my department to maritime studies, with Edgerton on the faculty. All of this produced gratifying results. Linder's thesis consisted of translating, analyzing, and annotating all the Ugaritic texts dealing with ships and the sea. He later founded the Department of Marine Archaeology at Haifa University, where I later served as Visiting Professor of Maritime Civilizations in the spring semester of 1993.

For his part, Doc offered courses on sonar and on strobe photography. One of his courses trained students in the use of sonar by taking them out in a boat on the Charles River and mapping the Callahan Tunnel by sonar. This expedition was valuable and effective, but it did produce a comic side-effect.

From some unknown source, possibly jealous colleagues, Charles Schottland, the acting president heard an unfavorable account of our exercise. So he summoned me to his office and proceeded to upbraid me: "If what I have heard is true, you are doing something disgraceful. You are giving graduate credit for charting the Callahan Tunnel when everyone knows where it is!" I explained that our program was designed to train marine archaeologists. An important part of their training was learning how to use sonar to detect underwater objects, including ancient shipwrecks. Without practical experience operating the equipment, our Ph.D. graduates would be unqualified to take professional jobs as marine archaeologists. I succeeded in restoring peace with Schottland, but I wished that more university administrators would have enough sense to realize that it was their business to facilitate, and not hamper, the work of competent faculty. Charley once told me that administrators should receive much higher salaries than scholars because the latter love their work, whereas administrators do not.

The high point of our social life in Brookline, where I lived at this time, was provided by Dr. Jack Fein, chief of surgery at the Beth Israel Hospital. He was hated by his staff and was, by all accounts, not a very good surgeon. Actually, Jack scorned surgery and once told me that he could teach a muzhik to perform an appendectomy in two hours. But Jack was a unique personality among the Boston intelligentsia. He gave parties at his charming home in South Brookline. Jack had an uncanny gift for spotting talented people in many different fields. It was not unusual to find two or three Nobel laureates at his soirees. At the same time he could spot talent in young people whom the world had not yet discovered. He also knew that a successful party needed a few "ordinary" folks who were happy to be in brilliant company and just listen and admire. An assemblage of geniuses with no one to adore them can only add up to a social disaster.

There were many attractive features of Jack's home. He had a notable library, a magnificent collection of music, and a garden on which he lavished much care. For example, he made annual trips to Holland to procure the choicest of bulbs. The ambiance was of his creation. There were, however, less beautiful aspects of his menage. His housekeeper was an unattractive old woman who did more than run the kitchen. She managed the house. Jack would inform her of the guest list of every party, but he never told his wife a thing, not even when he planned a party and whom he was inviting. She felt, and was, outranked by the old housekeeper in the hierarchy of the household.

The entertainment at his parties included monologues by Jack himself. They would often include amusing tales translated from Yiddish originals. Jack enjoyed having a captive audience. The quality of the celebrities among the guests provided conversation that was unsurpassed in the halls of Harvard and M.I.T. What a treat it was to hear Gershom Sholem discuss Jewish mysticism or Roman Jakobson hold forth on any aspect of linguistics or literature. After Jack died, a memorial service honoring his memory was held at Harvard, in a hall that held about four hundred people. Those present included the cream of the Cambridge establishment. But without Jack's presence, the age of his salon came to an abrupt end. Those of us who recall that age had never known anything like it before and doubt that its like will ever recur.

Jack Fein was an interesting man who engaged in interesting research projects. For example, he collected horseshoe crabs on the beaches and did research on their possible value for curing serious diseases. He was a fellow of the American Academy of Arts and Sciences. He entered my name for election as a fellow and kept resubmitting it until I was elected. Jack recognized that I needed to mingle and exchange ideas with gifted scholars. If I had resided in England, my honorary fellowship in the Royal Asiatic Society would have filled that need. Although I am financially unable to participate in the meetings in London, I appreciate my association with the Royal Asiatic Society, especially since they elected me for the right reasons, namely, my contributions in Ugaritic, Minoan, and comparative Semitics.

When I joined the AAAS, monthly meetings were held at the Brandige estate, near my home in Brookline. Later they were held in the building in Cambridge conceived and given to the Academy by Edwin Land, the founder of the Polaroid Company. The monthly meetings, which include a reception, lecture, and dinner, provide social events of some value, but more meaningful to me are the weekly lunches. They are attended by about thirty or forty fellows who meet to discuss their ideas and listen to the ideas of others. They have no agenda, and intellectual fellowship is the order of the day.

At one of the weekly lunches, Victor Weisskopf, who was then president of the Academy, informed me that he was about to leave for Rome to serve on a papal advisory council discussing the problem of global overpopulation. Victor wanted to know the biblical basis of the church's view. I told him that the first commandment in Genesis is, "Be fruitful and multiply, and fill the earth." "That is just the trouble," he responded. "We have filled the earth." I had never considered that before, and I observed that it is the only biblical commandment that the human race has fully obeyed. Such are the results of personal contacts at small gatherings of the AAAS.

Another personal contact that benefited me at this time was my relationship with George Hanfmann. I met George through Miriam Balmuth, who had studied with me in a summer program at Brandeis and went on to get her doctoral degree under Hanfmann.[36] She told him about my work, and eventually he and I became friends. I once told him about my decipherment of Ugaritic and the trouble I was having with Albright. He responded, "You can't teach an old dog new tricks."

When Hanfmann came to the United States from Germany, he already had a Ph.D. Being an astute man, he recognized the avenue to success here and went to Johns Hopkins for a second Ph.D., this one under David Robinson. For his thesis, Hanfmann produced a volume on Robinson's excavations at Olynthus. In return, Robinson secured him a tenured position at Harvard. Later Hanfmann excavated at Sardis in Turkey, funded by a society that he organized, The Friends of Sardis.

It was Hanfmann who was invited to submit names of scholars for selection in Marquis's *Who's Who in America*. This came at a good time, and I ended up being listed, not only in *Who's Who in America,* but also in *World's Who's Who in Science,* which categorized archaeology as a science. All of this was picked up by many like volumes at home and abroad. George Hanfmann gave me a big boost in my professional career.

During my Brandeis years, I led yearly archaeological study tours to various regions, including the Near East, North Africa, and the Mediterranean. The people on these trips were, for the most part, interested in learning, as was I. To that end, I assigned an extensive reading list before we left and lectured on the civilizations and the sites we were visiting. I did not encourage shopping, although occasionally participants enjoyed either a free morning or afternoon. I remember that in Crete, mornings were devoted to archaeological sites and late afternoons to swimming.

On one of these trips, I visited Robert Graves in his estate at Deya on the island of Majorca. My talented and famous cinema friend, Albert Lewin, had introduced Graves and me, and Graves had written the favorable blurb for the jacket of my *Before Columbus*. Through it all, Graves and I became good friends. During this visit, Graves asked me how I explained the awareness of the Central Americans concerning matters on the other side of the Atlantic. I replied, "Through contact by ships." Graves politely disagreed with me and attributed that awareness to the effects of hallucinatory mushrooms that expanded the minds of the early Central Americans. Our conversation strengthened my suspicion that Graves received his inspiration partly from drugs.

Graves's mystical side came out during the same visit. He had a signet ring with an inscription. He told me it was the official ring of an ancestor of his, a general of Alexander the Great who had remained in Afghanistan

---

[36] Miriam Balmuth is Professor of Archaeology at Tufts University. Her specialty is Sardinia.

as king of a city-state. I told Graves that the inscription was in Arabic letter forms that never appeared before Islam, which arose in the seventh century C.E. Graves respected my knowledge. He knew quite a bit of Latin and Greek but was unfamiliar with orientalia, such as Arabic. Thus, he accepted the factual veracity of what I said but was jolted by the sudden disappearance of his royal descent from a king in Afghanistan. I am sorry I felt obliged to shatter a glamorous illusion.

I was with my wife, Joan, when I visited Graves in Deya. As she and I departed in a taxi for the city of Majorca in the late afternoon, Graves tossed a rose through the open rear window, into her lap. She cherished the rose and kept it pressed in a book. A few days later, however, a chambermaid threw the dried petals into the trash while we were out of the room. Joan felt about as badly as Graves did when he lost his illusions of royal descent. Graves was a poet and had said good-bye to a lady, with a rose, as befits a poet.

The tours to Central Asia, Greece, Italy, Spain, Meso-America, South America, and other similar regions were preparing me for the study of long-range, global cultural diffusion. During my final years at Brandeis, I did extensive research into pre-Columbian connections between the Old and New Worlds. So it was that I had occasion to study a work called the Popul Vuh. Around 1550 C.E., an educated Mayan wrote this work in the Mayan language but in the Latin-Spanish alphabet. It is a sort of pagan Mayan Bible giving the history and mythology of the mountain Mayans in what is now Guatemala.

The authenticity of the Popul Vuh, in the sense that it contains ancient material that could not have been supplied by the Spanish missionaries, is proved by its tale of the cosmic cause of toothache, namely, a worm that insists on eating human gums and refuses to accept the finest fruits instead. Accordingly, an incantation is provided to exorcise the worm and rid humankind of it, thus sparing us the pain of toothaches. In the Old World, the only known myth concerning the worm and toothaches was discovered in the nineteenth century; it is written in Mesopotamian cuneiform.[37]

The Popul Vuh also records that the authorization for establishing the Quiche Mayan nation came from the eastern shore of the Atlantic and that contacts with the mother country in the Old World were maintained for a while, contacts that periodically reconfirmed the authority to found the daughter colony in the New World. The scenario that emerges is that deep in pre-Columbian times there was contact between the eastern and western hemispheres. Just as texts and artifacts of the eastern hemisphere reflect trans-Atlantic contact, so do texts and artifacts of the western hemisphere. Our investigations are making it possible to embark on a global

---

[37] James B. Pritchard, ed., *ANET* (3d ed.; Princeton: Princeton University Press, 1969), pp. 100–101.

history of the world in which all the segments of the world had direct or indirect contact with each other since Neolithic times.

During the summer vacations I began to seek visiting professorships in various parts of the United States: the Ozarks, New Mexico, and Hawaii. I hoped to broaden my knowledge of my own country, for my regular positions had been limited to the Northeast, from Washington, D.C., to Massachusetts, though later they were extended to Dartmouth College in New Hampshire. These visiting professorships likewise added to my equipment for dealing with cultural diffusion.

The Brandeis years were full of varied connections, some of which reflected the galaxy of colleagues whom I brought in. I shall limit the long list to four very different scholars of merit: the Assyriologist Ernest R. Lacheman, the polymath Silvestro Fiore, the Egyptologist Louis Vico Žabkar, and the art historian Erwin Goodenough.

Early in my career I became involved in the study of the Nuzi tablets, which eventually associated me with Ernest R. Lacheman. The Nuzi tablets of the Amarna Age (1400–1200 B.C.E.) give us a more detailed knowledge of a community than we have of any community until fairly recent times. In fact, we know more about Nuzi than about Boston circa 1700. Lacheman, a French-speaking Swiss from Lausanne, came to Harvard for his Ph.D. While there, he had access to the Nuzi tablets in the Harvard Semitic Museum and went on to devote his life to them.

Lacheman and I jointly published an article on the month-names of the Nuzi calendar. He had been earning his living as the pastor of a French Congregational Church in Torrington, Connecticut, but later joined the faculty of the Department of Religion at Wellesley College, located near Brandeis University. Wellesley did not allow him to offer courses on Assyriology, but his infectious zeal for the Nuzi tablets attracted some of the Wellesley students to study with him outside of class for no academic credit. One of those students was Martha Morrison, who went on to earn a Ph.D. at Brandeis. As soon as I came to Brandeis, I established relations with Lacheman and, on his retirement at Wellesley, secured a faculty position for him at Brandeis. Finally, albeit late in his life, he could at last teach the subject he loved and train disciples in it.

Silvestro Fiore was an Italian born and raised in Tunisia. Fiore's father was a remarkable man. As an Italian in Tunisia, he was scorned by the French, but he persisted in sending Silvestro to French schools because they were the finest in Tunisia. Silvestro studied many subjects, including classical Arabic, with European scholars. His father approved of this but insisted that Silvestro also pursue Arabic at a Muslim *madrasa*, where Silvestro studied the Qur'an and other Islamic texts in accordance with traditional medieval methods. The Fiore family, although Roman Catholic, wanted to understand their Muslim neighbors on those neighbors' own terms. Silvestro went on to earn a doctorate in Europe, where he specialized in European languages and literatures. In America he received a faculty post at Brown University, where he did not feel at home intellectually. The fact that a colleague of Fiore's who specialized in the Renaissance did not know Latin and only decided to study first-year Latin after receiving tenure shocked Silvestro.

Fiore was admired by scholars in various fields. The breadth of his knowledge is reflected in his publication of a good, even successful, volume on Assyriology. Fiore liked my Department of Mediterranean Studies, and I saw in him a genuine Mediterranean scholar. Consequently, I secured for him a tenured position and enjoyed intellectual discussions with him. His stay at Brandeis was, for him, the first time in his life that he felt fulfilled as a teacher. Tragically, he soon became afflicted with melanoma and died. I missed him deeply. My consolation was that I brightened his last years by recognizing his worth and giving him the opportunity to teach at his proper high level.

I have never claimed to be an "Egyptologist's Egyptologist," but when Dropsie informed me that I was Professor of Assyriology and Egyptology, I took the title seriously and am satisfied with the results. During my decade at Dropsie, I always taught a course on some phase of Egyptian, whether Classical, Late, or Coptic. We always read texts in the original scripts: hieroglyphic, hieratic, and the varieties of Coptic. I also published contributions on Egypto-Semitic and turned out qualified Egyptologists, including William A. Ward. He spent the greater part of his career at the American University in Beirut, but eventually the political situation forced him to leave. Fortunately, he then joined the excellent Egyptological department at Brown University.

My labors also bore fruit in other ways. For example, one student, Loren R. Fisher, happened to have taken courses in Coptic with me at Brandeis. Then, as a professor at Claremont Colleges, he taught James Robinson Coptic. Robinson is the director of the important project on the Coptic gnostic papyri discovered in Egypt.[38] Against all this background, the reader will understand why I sought a full-time Egyptologist for the Department of Mediterranean Studies at Brandeis.

Naturally, I wanted an Egyptologist who could integrate the subject into the rest of the department. Dr. Louis Vico Žabkar (1914–1994), trained in Egyptology at the Oriental Institute of the University of Chicago, was just the person for this task. He was also interested in joining the Department of Mediterranean Studies at Brandeis. Žabkar was a Catholic priest teaching general history at Loyola College, a Jesuit institution in Chicago. He knew Latin, Greek, and Hebrew, and I explained that I wanted him to teach Egyptological

---

[38] James Robinson (b. 1924) received the D.Theol. at Basel (1952) and the Th.D. at Princeton Theological Seminary (1955). He has served as editor and translator of *The Nag Hammadi Library in English*. He has spent most of his career as a professor at Claremont Graduate School.

courses that interested him but to relate them to the other Mediterranean cultures that he knew. He assured me there would be no problem.

Žabkar did not wear priestly garb, and, although he was a faithful Catholic, he desired to be a professional full-time Egyptologist, not a clergyman. Soon after he joined my department in 1969, he asked to speak privately with me. It was at the start of the fall semester, in September. He told me he wanted to marry a young woman from Chicago whom he, as her family's priest, had known for many years. He wanted my permission to go ahead. I told him that I had no objection to his marriage, but I did not want to offend my Catholic friends, such as the Jesuits of the Pontifical Biblical Institute in Rome. Accordingly, I expressed the wish that he do everything properly and be officially laicized by the Catholic Church before he married. He assured me that he had already applied for laicization and he would soon have permission from Rome. The word "soon" was more optimistic than realistic. I asked him when he expected to hear from Rome, to which he replied, "Before Thanksgiving." Well, Thanksgiving passed, and then Christmas, and then New Year's. I was worried, but Žabkar was confident that nothing had gone awry. The delay simply reflected the heavy workload of the Vatican office processing requests by priests for lay status without abandoning their Catholic religion.

Around the start of the spring semester, the permit arrived from Rome, and Louis married the lovely and soulful Joan Karaganis in Chicago. Everything went smoothly during Žabkar's first year of teaching, but I was jolted by his policy for students who wished to study for more than one year of Egyptian with him. His rule was, "Love it or leave it." Žabkar felt that no serious student of Egyptology should be interested in anything else. His attitude might have fit in with the spirit then prevailing at the Oriental Institute in Chicago, but it was hardly in keeping with Mediterranean Studies. I did not put pressure on Žabkar, however, because he believed in what he was doing and I have never liked to cramp anyone's style, just as I have never allowed people to cramp mine. Furthermore, Žabkar was a masterful Egyptologist. He had a superb Egyptological library and, in addition to teaching well, he kept his hand in archaeological field work and published. I had no reason to ask him to change.

Žabkar did not retire until 1982, nine years after I left Brandeis as emeritus professor. By 1992 he was badly stricken with cancer. He clung to life wretchedly until September 1994. He did not want people to see him suffer, so I was among many who did not even know he was ill. I attended the mass for him in Rockport, Massachusetts, followed by his burial in the local cemetery. Louis and Joan were private people and lived in Rockport during their Brandeis years. Because they lived quite far from Boston, their social life with their professional colleagues was reduced to the barest minimum. Sadly, I was Žabkar's only Brandeis colleague at the funeral. Three of his Brandeis disciples also attended. His widow told me that I had fulfilled his life ambition to teach Egyptology full-time at the doctoral level and that I had brightened the final phase of his professional career. Among my best deeds are what I did for Lacheman, Fiore, and Žabkar.

The last of the four I am singling out is quite different from the other three. I brought Erwin Goodenough to Brandeis for only one year, after he had already completed a distinguished career at Yale University and published thirteen impressive volumes of his magnum opus on symbols in the Greco-Roman world. One of the sensational implications of his opus was that Hellenistic Judaism had borrowed pagan themes such as Leda and the Swan, which are actually carved on Jewish sarcophagi. Goodenough loved to shock "true believers," both Christian and Jewish. The conservative Jewish students put up with his provocative antics, albeit not gladly. Their Christian counterparts proved not as tolerant, and one of them (Edwin Yamauchi, who has turned out to be a very productive and versatile scholar) walked out of class in a huff. I did not understand Goodenough's abrasive attitude until he told me one day that he had been raised as a fundamentalist but had subsequently achieved secular enlightenment. Thereafter, his pleasure in life was tormenting "true believers."

Quite frankly, Goodenough was not a dedicated teacher at Brandeis. He would come to class unprepared. On one occasion he opened his class with the question, "Do any of you wish to inquire about anything?" No one raised a hand, whereupon Goodenough dismissed class with the words: "If you don't want to know anything, there is no point in holding class." Goodenough was an outstanding, accomplished scholar, but he added little or nothing to the program of Mediterranean Studies. His rebellion against fundamentalism was sophomoric, and his domestic life was stormy. The last of his three marriages took place during the period that he and I saw a great deal of each other in Boston. Soon after, he died of cancer, as he was desperately trying (alas, in vain) to complete a final article.

Still, I profited from some of my conversations with him. He made me aware of the difference between live symbols and dead symbols. For example, a woman who wears a cross on her necklace implies that she is a Christian, for in our culture the cross is a live symbol. However, someone can wear a *crux ansata,* the ancient Egyptian *ankh*-sign, without implying that she is a devotee of Pharaonic religion, because the *ankh*-sign is, at least in the mainstream of our culture, a dead symbol. This was but one of many insights that I gained through my contact with the four scholars alongside whom I served at Brandeis: Goodenough, Žabkar, Fiore, and Lacheman.

In 1973 I went on a lecture tour of the Far East. It began with Japan. Hirohito's youngest brother, Prince Mikasa, had invited me to be the guest speaker at the celebration of the Japan Near East Society's twentieth year. Prince Mikasa was the founder and president of the Society. I delivered my lectures in English, dividing them into sections that filled about ten minutes each. My gifted Japanese disciple, Professor David Toshio Tsumura, translated each section into Japanese when I came to the end of a ten-minute segment. Mikasa also arranged a tour of Japan's universities and other points of interest, including Hokaido, which is of interest for the study of the Ainu.

Leaving Japan, I flew to Hong Kong, where I was greeted by a former student, Professor Wilson Chow. Of all the Chinese students I taught, I found those from Hong Kong easiest to relate to. They had the Chinese virtue of working hard, plus familiarity with the English language and British methods of organization. In Hong Kong we visited restaurants featuring the cuisine of every part of China. Wilson and I had three meals together every day, savoring the cooking of three different regions. So in my stay of a week in Hong Kong, I enjoyed about twenty different traditions of cuisine. The variety there is comparable to that among the nations of Europe. There is no simpler way to avoid the pitfall of thinking of the Chinese in terms of a homogeneous unit than to savor the variety of their cuisine.

My last visit to ethnic Chinese territory on that lecture tour was Taiwan. Chiang Kai-shek had stripped mainland China of all its archaeological treasures and built a magnificent museum to house them on Taiwan. In addition, the Academia Sinica had moved from Communist China to Taiwan, so that the brains of China as well as its artistic and archaeological treasures were in Taiwan. My student in Taiwan had helpful contacts with the Academia Sinica and Museum directors and curators, as well as with the Christian colleges where he taught. Accordingly I gained prompt access to all the circles that interested me. I found the president of the Christian college, who was also Professor of New Testament Studies, particularly interesting. He had been raised in Taiwan, which was part of the Japanese Empire. During the Second World War he had piloted a Japanese combat plane. Although a believing Christian, he was also a loyal subject of Emperor Hirohito, whom he regarded as divine. After Japan lost the war, he heard Hirohito declare on the radio that he was not divine but quite human. This shook the very being of the Christian pilot. Until I heard this confession, I thought that no believing Christian could also think that any man other than Jesus could also be a god.

A member of the Academia Sinica gave me a bottle of "the finest wine" as a parting gift. The wine turned out to be colorless and about 100 proof (50 percent alcohol). I innocently drank a small glass and immediately saw double. It took several hours before I recovered my senses and normal vision. It seems that *wine* in Taiwan does not always mean what *wine* means in America and Europe, at least back in 1973.

Before returning to America, I presented several lectures in Melbourne and Sydney, Australia. In Melbourne I spoke at two universities: the state university of Victoria, and the privately endowed Monash University. Professor Harry Redner of Monash University was instrumental in arranging my lectures in Melbourne. In Sydney, I made contact with the University of New South Wales through a former student, Noel Weeks, who served as Professor of History there. The Semitist Alan Crown, one of the outstanding authorities on the Samaritans, was also at Sydney. Years later he played a role in catapulting me into the circle of Samaritanologists.

Back at home, things were not going as smoothly as they had on my tour. In the late 1960s and early 1970s, numerous universities faced a significant financial challenge. Brandeis was no different. Financial reality being what it is, the larger departments wielded more clout than the numerically small departments, which led the Brandeis administration to target three departments for destruction, even though they were productive and of high quality: History of Ideas, Linguistics, and Mediterranean Studies.

As early as 1970 I had begun looking for an escape hatch because mandatory retirement at the age of sixty-eight would arrive in 1976, when I would still have to support an ailing wife and five children of high-school and college age. It was then that I received a phone call from David Radovsky of New York University, head of an academically weak department of Hebraic Studies. Radovsky needed someone productive to bolster the quality of his department. Since professors at Brandeis were permitted to work one day a week elsewhere, I advised Radovsky that, if he would meet my terms, I could carry a half-time load of courses on one day a week. We came to an agreement, and I taught one day per week at N.Y.U. for three years (1970–1973).

It was, as events soon proved, a wise move. Without saying anything to me, one of the administrative offices of Brandeis announced on local radio that I would be kept on only until 1976, whereupon the Department of Mediterranean Studies would be abolished.

New York University

Considering my lame-duck status at Brandeis unacceptable, I took a five-year appointment that the Gottesman Foundation endowed for me at N.Y.U. Granted, it guaranteed only two years more than Brandeis offered, but it was subsequently renewed, and I ended up remaining at N.Y.U. for sixteen years as a full professor. Only then, when all of my children had completed their university education and were married, did I retire from N.Y.U., as emeritus in 1989.

At N.Y.U. I had fewer students than at Brandeis, and the curriculum was not as well suited to what I had to offer. Nevertheless, I look back on those years with a great deal of fondness and satisfaction. I first taught in the Department of Hebrew and Education, where I was expected to teach Hebrew. As time went on, I added courses in the cognate languages, including Egyptian, which was a noncredit or independent study course for motivated Ph.D. candidates. Most of my students were going on to pursue master's degrees, but a few, such as Meir Lubetski (Baruch College, City University of New York), Daniel Grossberg (State University of New York, Albany), and Gary Rendsburg (Cornell University), went on to earn their doctorates.

My best students at N.Y.U. have brought me considerable, and, in some ways, unique, satisfaction. Sharon Keller, for example, began to read my books when she was twelve years old. Her ambition to be my disciple was fulfilled when she completed her doctoral program as my final student, in 1989. Sharon is already a productive and original scholar who has a fine teaching record at Hebrew Union College, Baruch College, Hunter College, and N.Y.U.

Gary Rendsburg is my leading disciple in Hebrew linguistics and philology. He is a tenured professor at Cornell University, and his rapidly growing publication record is already impressive. In addition to teaching Hebrew and Bible, he covers Pharaonic Egyptian. He is also associated with me in editing the series of volumes entitled *Eblaitica.* In 1997, he and I jointly published *The Bible and the Ancient Near East,* as the fourth edition of my *Ancient Near East.*

Claire Gottlieb is in a class by herself among those who took doctorates with me. She and her husband, Milton Gottlieb, are able business partners. While Claire has no desire to hold an academic position, she needs to be immersed in scholarship and creative research to make her life meaningful.

As a teenager, Ktziah Spanier was bored in school, so she persuaded her family to let her drop out of school on the condition that she would dedicate an equivalent amount of time reading the classics of Hebrew and English literatures. An early marriage and business pursuits kept her from higher education, but once her children were grown, she signed up at the Gallatin School of N.Y.U., a flexible program that gave credit for various life experiences. There Ktziah heard of my courses from Shalom Goldman, and soon she found herself immersed in cuneiform texts. Through her courses (at N.Y.U., the New School, and Yale) and her papers on the status of women in Mesopotamia and the Bible, she is making a significant contribution to scholarship.

Meir Lubetski is a savant with an original turn of mind, which is illustrated in the way he decided to study with me. Lubetski was well trained in the Bible and rabbinics from his native land of Israel, and he had received a college degree in secular studies from Hebrew University in Jerusalem. However, he felt a need for doctoral training in Near East studies. Lubetski already held an academic position teaching Hebrew at Baruch College (City University of New York), and he wanted to make use of new discoveries emanating from the archaeological excavations in his courses. Since he was already established in the area with a home, children, and a wife, who had a satisfying job as a librarian at Stern College, Lubetski decided to investigate where he might pursue a doctorate in the New York City area.

Students may choose as a mentor someone who can procure for them a good scholarship, someone at a prestigious university, someone enjoying popularity in the field, or merely someone recommended by a friend. Lubetski took none of these approaches. After finding out from university catalogues who was offering graduate training in and around New York City, he went to the main branch of the New York Public Library, where there is, in the Oriental division, a catalogue of publications in which not only each author's books but also his or her articles are listed. Through this process he found that my bibliography, as well as the reviews of my works, indicated that I was the most advisable mentor for him.

When he became my student, in addition to reading texts with me, he paid attention to the general principles that I expressed in class. One such principle is that the background for any particular part of the Bible should be sought in the language, literature, and culture of the land in which that part of the Bible is set. Thus, background for the book of Esther is supplied by Iran, while background for the Mosaic period comes from Egypt. Currently Lubetski is making important discoveries by interpreting Isaiah's Egyptian prophecies against the background of Egyptian language, literature, and archaeology. Lubetski came to me for the right reasons and reacted constructively to my guidance. Needless to say, he has been a stimulating disciple from whom I have learned a lot. There is nothing banal about him.

On November 20, 1994, Lubetski, Claire Gottlieb, and Sharon Keller produced a magnificent tribute to me, entitled "A Scholar for All Seasons," at the combined annual meetings of the Association of the Professors of Hebrew, the Society of Biblical Literature, the American Schools of Oriental Research, and the American Academy of Religion. Among that vast multitude were hundreds of my colleagues, professional friends, and former students. I was frankly overwhelmed, and it took more than a week for me to recover from the excitement and return to normalcy. The large number of my disciples who attended included distinguished scholars in a host of different fields: Ugaritic, biblical studies, Semitics, Egyptology, history, Assyriology, Hittitology, archaeology, maritime civilizations, museum work, and other related subjects. It took a year of hard work for Lubetski and Gottlieb, plus many others who assisted them, to prepare this tribute, but it was a remarkable success.[39]

During the 1995 annual conference of the same societies, in my native city of Philadelphia, Lubetski, again aided by Claire Gottlieb, arranged further honors for me that eclipsed by far everything that had taken place in Chicago. The first event was the dedication to me of the March 1996 issue of *Biblical*

---

[39] A Festschrift edited by Lubetski, Gottlieb, and Keller appeared in 1998. It was entitled *Boundaries of the Ancient Near East: A Tribute to Cyrus H. Gordon* (JSOTSup 273; Sheffield: Sheffield Academic Press, 1998).

Archaeologist, which consisted of articles describing my contributions to various fields. Each article was written by a specialist in that particular field.

The front and back covers are handsome. On the back cover, under a color photograph of me, one finds the following tribute by David Hopkins, the editor of the journal:

> A Scholar for All Seasons. Philadelphia born in 1908. Cyrus H. Gordon has been a prolific and pioneering contributor to the study of the world of the Near East and entire Mediterranean, since he received his Ph.D. from the University of Pennsylvania in l930. Mentored by some of the discipline's great luminaries (James Montgomery, Max Margolis, W. F. Albright) he has joined their constellation. His uniquely broad command of ancient studies has issued forth in hundreds of publications, dozens of Ph.D. graduates and an abidingly fecund legacy of ideas.

The grand finale of the celebration was a banquet in the Egyptian Gallery of the University Museum, on whose expeditions I had served as field archaeologist and epigrapher between 1931 and 1935. Judith Rodin, president of the University of Pennsylvania, was away in Europe, but she sent the following message:

> Dr. Gordon, I want to say how pleased I am that your remarkable career in Biblical and Near Eastern studies began at the University of Pennsylvania. This is where you earned your undergraduate and graduate degrees. This is where you began to teach. In the intervening years, we have marveled at the depth and breadth of your scholarship. You have been a discoverer, an illuminator, and a creator of knowledge. Whether looking to the past, as you excavated the secrets of history, or to the future, as you inspired your students in their scholarly careers, you have been constant in your dedication to excellence. I am delighted to join my colleagues in welcoming you back this evening as a most distinguished member of the Penn family. The University shines with an added brilliance because of your extraordinary achievements. You have my admiration and warmest good wishes. Sincerely, Judith Rodin.

Such accolades cannot but help warm one's heart, but I take equal pride and satisfaction in the accomplishments of my students. Among my other successful doctoral students at N.Y.U. is Daniel Grossberg, a tenured professor at the Albany campus of the State University of New York. His teaching and publications are mainly on Hebrew language and literature, but he has also published articles on literary motifs. His latest article is on the attitude of Psalms toward nature.

Finally, Constance V. Wallace took her Ph.D. with me at N.Y.U. in 1988. Since 1986, when we married, she has been a partner in all my work.

In addition to being privileged to work with such fine students, I was also able to turn my attention to a new field during my N.Y.U years: the Ebla tablets, which were discovered during that time. I immediately sensed their importance because they constitute the largest corpus of texts from the Early Bronze Age in the entire world. They are a thousand years older than the tablets from Ugarit.

I gave a public lecture on the tablets at N.Y.U., and in the audience was David Rose, of the architectural and development company of Rose Associates. David Rose was in his eighties, retired and quite wealthy. After my lecture, he asked me whether the audience came because the Ebla studies were any sort of avenue to making money. I assured him that the interest in Ebla was purely intellectual and reflected a desire to better understand the origins of Western civilization. At that point David Rose spontaneously and immediately offered to support the study of Ebla under my direction, with the explanation, "This is the kind of scholarship I want to support. I am sick and tired of money-grubbing."

David Rose received no formal schooling after the age of eleven. But in addition to amassing a fortune, he was a life-long avid reader. He reminded me of an expression used by some people I met in the Ozarks, where in earlier times there had been no institutions of higher learning. They had an expression that would apply to Rose. Instead of referring to well-informed people as "educated," they would call them "book-read." Abraham Lincoln, for example, fit this category. He had only about one year of formal education in his entire life, but he was self-educated or "book read." So also was David Rose, but his generous gift established the Center for Ebla Research at N.Y.U. Receiving support for such a project through the well-known foundations would have been unlikely because their committees generally operate with standard lists of areas that have already become "acceptable."

When I entered the field of Eblaitica in 1982, it was not politically correct to point out Hebrew connections. Ebla is in Syria, then an enemy of Israel. It turns out that Eblaite is a Semitic lingua franca with East and West Semitic analogues. It took a decade of needless controversy and polemics before the study of Eblaite was depoliticized. The Center for Ebla Research, through its volumes of *Eblaitica* and the original contributions of scholars trained in the seminars of the Center, played a major role in setting Eblaite studies on their proper course. Pointing out analogues to Eblaite from any Egypto-Semitic language, including Hebrew, is no longer taboo.[40]

---

[40] "The Eblaite Language," in *Contacts Between Cultures* (ed. A. Harrak; Lewiston, N.Y.: Edwin Mellen, 1992), Pages 101–7.

7.
RETIREMENT

I continued to teach full-time at N.Y.U. until I passed my eighty-first birthday in 1989, when I then became professor emeritus of Hebrew and other Near East Languages and Literatures in the Graduate School of Arts and Science. I still continue to direct the Center of Ebla Research but refrain from allocating to myself remuneration for writing on the Eblaite language and/or for administrative and editorial work performed. Academia is full of litigious and ill-willed people, so I do all I can to avoid even the appearance of self-interest.

After retiring from teaching at N.Y.U. on September 1, 1989, I traveled once again to the Far East on a lecture tour. As before, I went first to Japan to deliver a talk to the Society for Near Eastern Studies there. It is housed with an impressive library that covers cuneiform studies, archaeology, and Arabic as well as Hebrew studies. The Prince has an office there, which I understand is his refuge away from the Imperial Palace. The palace protocol does not really interest the intellectual Mikasa. Because my visit fell within the year following Hirohito's death, there were no formal festivities. Instead, we were regaled at an intimate lunch for six persons: Mikasa; our host, Mr. Ichiguro; a former student, Professor David Toshio Tsumura; a Japanese friend of Ichiguro, who did not know English; Connie; and I. The food was French cuisine at its best. Mikasa discussed Connie's doctoral thesis, "Broken and Double Plural Formation in the Hebrew Bible," with her.

The most interesting part of the conversation was Mikasa's answer to Connie's question, "Why did an imperial prince of Japan decide to specialize in Hebrew?" He explained, "During World War II, I could not help seeing that the two most dynamic regions in the world were the Marxist Soviet Union and the Christian nations of Europe and America. Karl Marx was born into a Jewish family, while Christianity, taken on its own terms, is the fulfillment of the Hebrew Bible. I therefore wanted to learn as much as possible about the source of the dynamism of the world today." I relate this conversation to show how Mikasa thinks globally.

After our stay in Japan, Connie and I flew to Korea, where I had connections through former students. In a Seoul hotel, we met a Korean businessman who had been raised during the Japanese occupation of Korea. He asked us where we had been in the Far East, and we told him that we had been invited by Prince Mikasa to lecture in Japan. When we mentioned Mikasa's name, the Korean turned pale. He explained to us that in school he had learned that mentioning the name of anyone in the imperial ruling family was sacrilege that would kill the offender like a bolt of lightning. The Japanese occupation of Korea may be over, but its effects linger on.

While we were in Korea, I delivered a lecture at a large and influential Christian seminary. Its president, Jin Tae Lee, was a former student of mine. He had come to Brandeis to study for his doctorate under my tutelage during the palmy days when I could secure a good fellowship to cover his financial needs as well as those of his wife and their two young daughters. He came from an upper-class family, and, with doctorate in hand, he was destined to achieve great things. In time, he became an American citizen living in California, legally able to spend enough of every year in Seoul to preside over the seminary.

After my lectures, he had to remain at the seminary to supervise its activities, but his wife accompanied Connie and me to the ancient Korean capital of Kung Ju. On the train she told us of her life prior to her husband's studies at Brandeis. It seems that he needed five years of undergraduate schooling in America, but they could not afford to transport her and the two children to America. So they were separated for five years. She told us that she cried herself to sleep every night for five years but there never was any doubt in her mind that her husband's education came first. I tell this to impress upon my American readers some of the ideals and some of the differences between Far Easterners and Westerners. It helps explain, I believe, why the first generation of American-born East Asians continue to make increasing inroads into our intellectual elite.

Even in the midst of retirement, I did not stay entirely out of the classroom. Dartmouth College, for one, appointed me the Visiting Brownstone Professor of Hebrew in the Department of Asian Languages for the spring semester in 1990. There I was able to work on the same faculty as Shalom Goldman, who took his doctorate under my tutelage at N.Y.U. Finally, during the spring semester of 1993, I was the Visiting Hatter Professor of Maritime Civilizations at the University of Haifa, in the department founded by my student Dr. Elisha Linder. This latter appointment reflects my current concern with long-range cultural diffusion.

ONGOING RESEARCH

My main project, as I write in 1999, is this "working autobiography" showing how my varied investigations during the last seventy years fit together, helping to pave the way for the eventual composition of a global history of civilization: a task for future generations of scholars to continue.

As I complete this autobiographical sketch, I am still working on long-range cultural diffusion. There has been so much movement of populations due to trade, conquest, the search for a better life elsewhere, sheer adventure, and the like that none of us are aborigines in the land we call our own. Moreover, wherever a new population enters, an old population becomes dislocated so that the latter moves elsewhere, dislocating still others. Finally, the process of mingling to form hybrid populations with hybrid cultures continues ubiquitously. At various levels, this process has been in operation globally, by land and sea, since the Stone Age. The spread and hybridization of actually civilized humans and their cultures have been in progress since Neolithic times.

While the generalities just expressed provide a useful framework, they would be meaningless historically without specific examples. The two most striking and compelling illustrations that I have pointed out in recent publications involve the spread of the Near Eastern alphabet to China (ca. 1200 B.C.E.) and the spread of maritime Near Easterners to America in Imperial Roman and Byzantine times (ca. 100 to 500 C.E.). The sensational nature of such discoveries makes it all the more necessary to found our treatment of the subject on demonstrably cogent grounds.

In 1987, Victor Mair, a Sinologist at the University of Pennsylvania, asked me whether anything was taking place in the Near East around 1200 B.C.E. that could explain the fact that the earliest Chinese texts (on the oracle bones that suddenly appear at that time in the Shang Dynasty, at many sites) have twenty-two special graphs, like the twenty-two letters of the Phoenician or Hebrew alphabets. There is also a twenty-two-letter Ugaritic alphabet, which was found away from the city-state, at Beth Shemesh and Mount Tabor. Mair thought that the numerical identity was more than a mere coincidence.

I informed Mair that 1200 B.C.E. fell precisely during the period when the twenty-two-letter alphabet was spreading through and beyond the Near East. Gradually it came to light that several basic uses of the twenty-two graphs in the Near and Far East are indeed the same. In both regions the twenty-two graphs are used (1) calendrically, (2) as a numbering system, (3) for arranging or ordering (alphabetizing), and (4) probably also for phonetic spelling. Quite striking is the fact that forms of some of the twenty-two Chinese graphs are exactly the same shape as specific Ugaritic, but not Mesopotamian, cuneiform letters. Therefore, one can conclude that the twenty-two-letter alphabet was diffused from the Near to the Far East by 1200 B.C.E.

Most of the Ugaritic texts are written in an alphabet consisting of twenty-nine letters (plus a thirtieth, which duplicates the nineteenth phonetically) arranged in the same order as they have come down to us today. This is due to the fact that the alphabet also served as a lunar calendar. A lunar month consists of approximately twenty-nine and one-half days. For practical considerations, the calendar has to reckon with whole days and not with fractions of days. Therefore, some months have twenty-nine days, while others have thirty. Thus, the Ugaritic alphabet has twenty-nine phonetically distinctive letters plus an extra thirtieth.

In *The Alphabet and the Ancient Calendar Signs,* Hugh A. Moran sensed that the ancient calendars were spread throughout the eastern hemisphere by ancient merchants. David N. Kelley later observed that those calendars also came from Central America, notably from the Mayan sphere.[41]

In the Belen district southwest of Albuquerque, New Mexico, carved into the living rock at the entrance to a ravine leading up to a site with ruined structures, one finds an abridged version of the Ten Commandments in the old Phoenician-Hebrew-Samaritan script. I knew of this inscription, but it was not until my wife Connie and I saw, in the Israel Museum, two stone plaques with abbreviated Ten Commandments, labeled "Samaritan Mezzuzot," that I could make any sense of it. Such Decalogue Stones are typical only of Samaritan communities.

To survive in the Diaspora, the Samaritans and Jews often soft-peddled their ancient enmities and made common cause. Although they had what we today call denominational differences, they correctly regarded each other as Israelites of the same Mosaic faith devoted to the worship of Yahweh. The Samaritan cultic center is Mount Gerizim, near Shechem/Nablus, whereas the Jews claim that Jerusalem is the true cultic center of Israel. But in the Diaspora the two sects believed that their ethnic kinship was so close that they influenced each other.

All this takes on great interest when one considers an archaeological find near Newark, Ohio. There excavators uncovered a small cult object with an abridged Decalogue that resembles the abridged Ten Commandments of the Samaritans. There are, to be sure, differences. The Newark Decalogue is written in a strange but unmistakable form of the later script of the Jews. It

---

[41] See the second edition of *The Alphabet and the Ancient Calendar Signs* under the joint authorship of Moran and Kelley (1969).

opens with a likeness of Moses with his name (MŠH "Moses") spelled out over the image. All this is very un-Jewish. Among the Samaritans, however, Moses is somewhat like Jesus among the Christians. For the Jews, while Moses remains the foremost prophet, he is but one of many biblical prophets. An autobiography is not the place to expatiate on this topic. Suffice it to point out that the Samaritans, unlike the Jews, celebrate the *Molad Mosheh* ("the birthday of Moses"), which is to be compared typologically with the Christmas of Christendom.

Moreover, it is significant that, in 390 C.E. Theodosius the Great regulated the law obliging the combined Jewish-Samaritan community to supply the Roman state with ships to transport goods and personnel. This shows that the Jews and Samaritans had a well-known naval capability. Of course, they could have reached America only in ships, but the fact that the Jewish-Samaritan community was able to shoulder the navicular function (*navicu laria functio*, "the duty of supplying and operating ships for the state") indicates that they had both the vessels and the naval personnel to do so.

The simplest route from the Mediterranean to the site of the Decalogue Stone in New Mexico would be across the Atlantic, into the Gulf of Mexico, up the Rio Grande, and finally up its tributary the Rio Puerco to the site of the Stone.

An indispensable factor in my involvement in such fields as Sinology was my reputation as an open-minded scholar, which is why Victor Mair consulted me about the twenty-two Chinese graphs. Meanwhile I sensed that northern India may have lain on what later became known as the Silk Route, along which route Northwest Semites had exerted the cultural impact that ultimately reached China. Being traders, they had to keep records, which accounts for their transmission of the twenty-two "alphabetic" glyphs to China. A single, giant jump from Canaan to China is out of the question. The Desi words in Bengali, however, point, if not to *the* route, at least to *a* route of the transmission.

My prior awareness of Indology was positive but limited in actual training at the University of Pennsylvania. Montgomery had advised me to take a year of Sanskrit in order to understand and appreciate the importance of the subject for linguistic science. I did so, in 1929–1930, and was the only student in the class, which was taught by W. Norman Brown. Whitney's *Sanskrit Grammar* and Lanman's *Sanskrit Reader* were the textbooks I used. Devanagari was the script I learned. One does not become an Indologist by studying Sanskrit for a year, but I became and remained interested in India, as is, for example, indicated by my 1958 article on "Indo-European and Hebrew Epic" in the Benjamin Mazar Festschrift.

One of my students at N.Y.U., Dr. Nelly Segal, never discussed India with me, but she knew of my open-mindedness and wide range of interests. Nelly, who works in the Rutgers University library and teaches

Hebrew courses at Monmouth College whenever students request courses on that language, lives in Tinton Falls, New Jersey. Nearby, in Eatontown, lives a Bengali scholar, Liny Srinivasan, Ph.D., who has made an important discovery that her Indologist acquaintances refuse to take seriously.

Liny had been working for twelve years on the problem of "Desi" words in Bengali. The native Indian savants had long recognized that much of the Bengali vocabulary is not of Sanskrit derivation but is, in fact, quite foreign to the entire Indo-European family of languages. They call such words Desi, which means "primitive or uncouth," and attribute them to unidentified primitive, prehistoric aborigines. Liny, however, connected the Desi words with the people of a land called "Kenyan" in Old Bengali texts. She, moreover, correctly identified Kenyan with Canaan, the land of the Hebrews. Accordingly, she began to seek the Desi words in Hebrew dictionaries and Ugaritic vocabulary lists, where she found so many striking similarities that she became convinced that the Desi words were Canaanite.

Finding little support among Indologists, she decided to find a Hebraist who might guide her. Because Liny lived in Eatontown, near Monmouth College, she inquired there and was told that Nelly Segal was the only authority on Hebrew at Monmouth. Liny showed Nelly her material, who said that it looked promising but that only an experienced Hebraist could render a meaningful opinion. Although Nelly had taken only a few of my courses over a decade earlier, she advised Liny to show me her material. When she did, I was immediately impressed, for if only a fraction of her striking identifications were correct, she had made an important discovery.

I arranged to have an avant-garde linguistic journal, produced by bold but fully accredited scholars, publish an article establishing Liny's priority of discovery.[42] Thus, under the joint authorship of Liny and me, *Mother Tongue* published an article that I wrote demonstrating the validity of her discovery. The implications of her discovery are far-reaching, including the fact that the Canaanites and Indo-Europeans were in touch with each other since about 2,000 B.C.E.

When Ezekiel reminded the people of Jerusalem, "Your father was (the West Semitic) Amorite, and your mother (the Indo-European) Hittite" (16:3), he knew whereof he spoke. From the start (e.g., Gen 23) the biblical tradition has Abraham dealing with Hittites. To state the situation somewhat differently, the basic genetic formula of the Hebrews was: Northwest Semites + Indo-European Hittites.

---

[42] I have prepared a study of the Near Eastern factors in the Rigveda, the oldest of the Sanskrit classics. The evidence consists largely of place names, names of deities, and technical terms. See "The Near East Background of the Rigveda," in *Ancient Egyptian and Mediterranean Studies in Memory of William A. Ward* (ed. L. Lesko; Providence: Dept. of Egyptology, Brown University, 1998), 117–20.

My modus operandi is straightforward. First, make sure your facts are right. Then, when you have weighed all the evidence from the primary sources and found that the consensus is wrong, scrap the consensus and follow the evidence. In most cases, your conclusion will be based on evidence that includes facts that had not been factored into the formulation of the consensus.

This invites not only bitter criticism but also rude as well as illogical denial. Should you take such an impolitic step? If you are untenured and married, with a spouse and children who depend on you for food, clothing, and shelter, you cannot afford to run the risk. But if you are driven by the quest for truth, you will shout your discovery from the rooftops without counting the cost. I did so long before I had tenure or given those hostages to fortune: wife and children. I have somehow survived, for which I thank a merciful Providence.

I am grateful for the gift of still breaking, now in my ninety-second year, new ground in the never-ending quest for formulating a unified history of humanity. And I am enjoying every minute of it.

My wise father told me that his fondest prayer was that his mind should not give out before his body. He published his longest book, just under a thousand pages, at the age of ninety and kept with up his research and writing until he was ninety-three. Then he devoted his time to setting his house in order, so as not to depart this life with his estate in disarray. He died peacefully in his sleep at the age of ninety-five. 'Alav ha-shalom!

I am grateful to my parents: to my Victorian mother who taught me always to do my best, because anything worth doing had to be done well; and to my father, physician and Hebraist, who inculcated a love of tradition along with the spirit of scientific enlightenment, each in its proper place.

It was they who prepared me for my distinguished teachers, so that I might be worthy of my teachers' long catena of scholarly tradition. I have been fortunate in reaching this point in my studies. In doing so, I have trained between eighty and ninety scholars for a Ph.D. and launched them in their academic careers in a wide range of fields. I have also raised five children, who have transmitted my values to my ten grandchildren. I have a wife who understands me and my work, and helps me at every turn. Could anyone ask for more?

APPENDIX A:
LIST OF DOCTORAL STUDENTS

The following register of doctoral students is arranged in alphabetical order by last name of student. Each entry includes the title of a student's dissertation, the institution where and the year when a dissertation was completed, and, when known, a student's past or current professional position. Note that some students completed dissertations under the direction of other advisors, which is indicated by placing an advisor's name prior to the granting institution.

Sally Ahl, Epistolary Texts From Ugarit: Structural and Lexical Correspondences in Epistles in Akkadian and Ugaritic (Brandeis, 1973)

Carl E. Armerding, The Historical Ages of Greece and Israel: A Literary-Historical Comparison (Harry Hoffner, Brandeis, 1968)

Lerdahl Michal Artzy, The Origin of the Palestinian Bichrome Ware (Ian Todd, Brandeis, 1972) University of Haifa

Michael Astour, Helleno-Semitica (Brandeis, 1962) University of Illinois, Edwardsville, Prof. of History

Ralph Beich, Nuzu Last Wills and Testaments (Brandeis, 1963)

Andrew Charles Bowling, Syntactical Examination of Clause Function in Late-Egyptian Narrative (Dwight Young, Brandeis, 1962)

J. Marvin Breneman, Nuzi Marriage Tablets (Ernest Lacheman, Brandeis, 1971)

Ellis R. Brotzman, The Plurality of the "Soul" in the Old Testament With Special Attention Given to the Use of Nefesh (NYU, 1987) Tyndale

Stephen Brown, The Serpent Charms of Ugarit (Brandeis, 1974)

Frederic W. Bush, A Grammar of the Hurrian Language (Brandeis, 1964) Fuller Theological Seminary, Retired

Wilson Chow, Kings and Queens of Nuzi (Ernest Lacheman, Brandeis, 1973)

Bert DeVries, The Style of Hittite Epic and Mythology (Harry Hoffner, Brandeis, 1967)

David H. Engelhard, Hittite Magical Practices: An Analysis (Harry Hoffner, Brandeis, 1970)

Loren Fisher, Nuzu Geographical Names (Brandeis, 1959)

Milton Fisher, The Lexical Relationship Between Ugaritic and Ethiopic (Brandeis, 1969)

David Freeman, Biblical Ideas of Paradise in the Light of Comparative Religion (Dropsie, 1951)

Fawsi Fahim Gadallah, Taxation and Corvee in Coptic Documents (Dropsie, 1956)

Mark Geller, Joshua ben Perahia and Jesus of Nazareth: Two Rabbinic Magicians (Brandeis, 1974) University College, London

George Giacumakis, The Akkadian of Alalakh (Dwight Young, Brandeis, 1963)

Shalom Goldman, The Joseph Story in Jewish and Islamic Lore (NYU, 1986) Emory University

Claire Gottlieb, Varieties of Marriage in the Bible: And Their Analogues in the Ancient World (NYU, 1989)

Daniel Grossberg, Nominalization in Biblical Hebrew (NYU, 1977) SUNYA

Gregory Hagg, The Interrelationship Between the New Testament and Tannaitic Judaism (NYU, 1988)

Victor P. Hamilton, Syriac Incantation Bowls (Gordon Newby, Brandeis, 1970)

Clyde Harrington, Assyro-Hebraic Relations in Sargonid Times 721–605 B.C. (Dropsie, 1953)

John Hartley, Studies in the Sahidic Version of the Apophthegmata Patrum (Brandeis, 1969) California State at Azusa

Thomas Charles Hartman, The Kadesh Inscriptions of Ramesses II: An Analysis of the Verbal Patterns of a Ramesside Royal Inscription (Dwight Young, Brandeis, 1967)

Roy E. Hayden, Court Procedure at Nuzu (Brandeis, 1962) Oral Roberts University

Walter Herzberg, Polysemy in the Hebrew Bible (NYU, 1979) Pardes Institute, Jerusalem

Harry A. Hoffner, Jr., The Laws of the Hittites (Brandeis, 1963) Univeristy of Chicago

Yulssus Lynn Holmes, The Foreign Relations of Cyprus During the Late Bronze Age (Brandeis, 1969)

Paul Hoskisson, The Deities and Cult Terms in Mari: An Analysis of the Textual Evidence (Martha Morrison, Brandeis, 1986) Brigham Young

David K. Huttar, Conditional Sentences in Coptic (Dwight Young, Brandeis, 1962)

Charles Isbell, Corpus of the Aramaic Incantation Bowls (Brandeis, 1973)

Walter C. Kaiser, Jr., The Ugaritic Pantheon (Brandeis, 1973) President, Gordon-Conwell

Joseph Kaster, The Archaeological Background of the Ugaritic Texts (Dropsie, 1954)

Sharon R. Keller, Egyptian Letters to the Dead in Relation to the Old Testament and Other Near Eastern Sources (NYU, 1989) Adjunct HUC, NYU, Baruch, Hunter

Timothy Kendall, Warfare and Military Matters in the Nuzi Tablets (Ernest Lacheman, Brandeis, 1974) Curator, Boston Museum of Fine Arts

Joseph N. Kickasola, Sahidic Coptic (N) ... AN Negation Patterns: A Morpho-Syntactic Description of Sentences and Adjuncts (Louis Jabkar, Brandeis, 1975)

Dennis F. Kinlaw, A Study of the Personal Names in the Akkadian Texts From Ugarit (Dwight Young, Brandeis, 1967) College president, Sewanee

Meredith Kline, The Ha-BI-ru (Dropsie, 1955) Gordon-Conwell

William Sanford LaSor, Semitic Phonemes: With Special Reference to Ugaritic and in Light of Egyptian Evidence (Dropsie, 1949) Fuller Theological Seminary

John Lawrenz, The Maritime Theme in Second Temple Numismatics (Brandeis, 1973)

Jin Tae Lee, The Ugaritic Numeral and Its Use As a Literary Device (Brandeis, 1973) Korea

Baruch A. Levine, Survivals of Ancient Canaanite in the Mishnah (Brandeis, 1962) NYU, Ben Gurion University

Arthur H. Lewis, Ugaritic Place-Names (Brandeis, 1966)

Timothy Tao-liang Lin, Egyptian and Its Hebraic Affinities (Dropsie, 1954)

Elisha Linder, The Maritime Texts of Ugarit: A Study in Late Bronze Age Shipping (Brandeis, 1970) University of Haifa, Center for Maritime Studies

Meir Lubetski, Maritime Horizons of the Jews in the Talmudic Period (NYU, 1976) Baruch College, Prof. of Languages

Donald H. Madvig, A Grammar of the Royal Assyrian Annals of the Sargonid Dynasty (Dwight Young, Brandeis, 1966)

L. N. Manross, The Combinatory Method in Ugaritic Exegesis (Dropsie, 1950)

Howard Marblestone, Dictys Cretensis: A Study of the Ephemeris Belli Troiani As a Cretan Pseudepigriphon (Brandeis, 1970) Lafayette College

Charles McDowell, Parallels Between Ancient Greek and Hebrew Poets (Brandeis, 1965)

Martha Morrison, Shilwa-Teshup: Portrait of a Hurrian Princess (Ernest Lacheman, Brandeis, 1974) Boston College

James Moyer, The Concept of Ritual Purity Among the Hittites (Harry Hoffner, Brandeis, 1969) Southwest Missouri State University

David Neiman, Patriarchal Institutions: A Study of the Social Institutions in the Patriarchal Period in the Light of Cuneiform Sources (Dropsie, 1955)

Gordon D. Newby, Ibn 'Asbat's Ta'rikh [With Edited Manuscript Text in Arabic] (Joseph DeSomgye, Brandeis, 1966) Emory

John Newell Oswalt, The Concept of Amon-Re As Reflected in the Hymns and Prayers of the Ramesside Period (Brandeis, 1968)

David Owen, The Loan Documents From Nuzu (Harry Hoffner, Brandeis, 1969) Cornell, Chair in History and Archaeology

Charles Pfeiffer, Neo-Babylonian Documents in the John Frederick Lewis Collection of the Free Library of Philadelphia (Dropsie, 1953)

Leon Picon, A Linguistic Analysis of the Sinuhe Romance (Dropsie, 1951)

William H. C. Poe, The Ceramic Technology of the Prehistoric Cultures of El-Khalil (Hebron): A Methodological Study Based Upon the Evidence of the 1964 and 1965 Seasons (Philip Hammond, Brandeis, 1971)

Arthur W. Poulton, The Martial Poetry of Greece and Israel (Brandeis, 1971)

Anson Frank Rainey, The Social Stratification of Ugarit (Brandeis, 1963) Tel Aviv University

Svi Rin, Acts of the Gods: The Ugaritic Epic Poetry (Brandeis, 1958) University of Pennsylvania (deceased)

Esther H. Roshwalb, "Build-up and Climax" in Ugaritic Literature With Biblical Parallels and Its Bearing on Biblical Studies (NYU, 1988)

William H. Rossell, A Handbook of Aramaic Magical Texts (Dropsie College, 1952) Southwestern Baptist Seminary (deceased)

Nahum Sarna, Studies in the Language of Job (Brandeis, 1955) Brandeis

Jack Sasson, Northernmost Syria: A Survey of Its Institutions Before the Fall of Mari (ca. 1757 B.C.) (Harry Hoffner, Brandeis, 1966) University of North Carolina Chapel Hill (retired)/Vanderbilt

John F. X. Sheehan, Studies in the Perfect With Waw in Pentateuchal Prose: Reexamination of the Accent Shift and Related Problems (Brandeis, 1968) Marquette University

Elmer Smick, Cuneiform Documents of the Third Millennium in the John F. Lewis Collection in the Public Library of Philadelphia (Dropsie, 1951) Gordon-Conwell (deceased)

Ktziah Spanier, Aspects of Fratriarchy in the Old Testament (NYU, 1989) New School for Social Research

Robert R. Stieglitz, Maritime Activity in Ancient Israel (Brandeis, 1971) Rutgers

Harold Stigers, Achaemenian Tablets in the John Frederick Lewis Collection of the Philadelphia Free Library (Dropsie, 1953)

Stephen C. Stohlman, Real Adoption at Nuzi (Ernest Lacheman, Brandeis, 1972)

Gerald Gordon Swaim, A Grammar of the Akkadian Tablets Found at Ugarit (Ernest Lacheman, Brandeis, 1962)

David Toshio Tsumura, The Ugaritic Drama of the Good Gods: A Philological Study (Brandeis, 1973) Japan Bible Seminary

Roy Uyechi, A Study of Ugaritic Alphabetic Personal Names (Brandeis, 1961)

Constance Wallace, Broken and Double Plural Formations in the Hebrew Bible (NYU, 1988)

Wiber Wallis, Aramaic and Mandean Magic and Their Demonology (Dropsie, 1955)

William Ward, A Comparative Study of Egyptian and Ugaritic Phonetics and Lexicography (Brandeis, 1958) American University of Beirut, Prof. of History and Archaeology/Brown University (deceased)

Carl Philip Weber, The Foreign Relations of Ugarit (Brandeis, 1966)

Noel K. Weeks, The Real Estate Interests of a Nuzi Family (Ernest Lacheman, Brandeis, 1972) University of Sydney, NSW Australia, Prof. of History

Marvin Russell Wilson, Syntactical Studies of Future Tenses in Sahidic (Dwight Young, Brandeis, 1963) Gordon College

Herbert Wolf, The Apology of Hattusilis (Harry Hoffner, Brandeis, 1967)

Jak Yakar, The Religious Architecture and Art of Early Anatolia (Philip Hammond, Brandeis, 1968) University of Tel Aviv, Prof. of Anatolian Archaeology

Edwin Yamauchi, Mandaean Incantation Texts (Brandeis, 1964) Miami University of Ohio, Prof. of History

Dwight Young, The Coptic Tenses in the Writings of Shenoute (Dropsie, 1955)

Frederick Young, The Epic of Baal and Anath: With Special Reference to Old Testament Literary Parallels (Dropsie College, 1954) Central Baptist Seminary, Kansas City, Kansas

G. Douglas Young, The Structure of the Poetry of Ugarit (Dropsie, 1948) Bible Institute, Jerusalem (deceased)

Gordon Young, The Historical Background of Phoenician Expansion Into the Mediterranean in the Early First Millennium B.C. (Brandeis, 1970) Purdue University, History

APPENDIX B:
BIBLIOGRAPHY OF WORKS

This bibliography is arranged by category to facilitate ease of use. Within each category, books and articles are arranged chronologically, while reviews are ordered alphabetically by last name of author.

Ancient Near East: History and Institutions

Books

Introduction to Old Testament Times. Ventnor, N.J.: Ventnor Publishers, 1953.
The World of the Old Testament. Garden City, N.Y.: Doubleday, 1958.
Het Oude Testament in historisch perspectief. Utrecht: Het Spectrum, 1959.
Il vecchio testamento e i popoli del mediterraneo orientale. Brescia: Morcelliana, 1959.
Geschichtliche Grundlagen des Alten Testaments. Zurich: Benziger, 1961.
The Ancient Near East. New York: W. W. Norton, 1965.

Articles

"Sabbatical Cycle or Seasonal Pattern? (Reflections on a New Book)," *Orientalia* 22 (1953): 79–81.
"Language As a Means to an End," *Antiquity* 29 (1955): 147–49.
"Colonies and Enclaves in Near East Antiquity." Pages 409–19 in *Studi orientalistici in onore di Giorgio Levi Della Vida.* Vol. 1. Pubblicazioni dell'Istituto per l'Oriente 52. Rome: Instituto per l'Oriente, 1956.
"The Role of the Philistines," *Antiquity* 30 (1956): 22–26.
"Ḥayye ha–Ruaḥ we–Ḥayyee ha–Yeṣira has–Sifrutit (Spiritual Life and Literary Creativity)." Pages 177–83, 342 in *Ha–Historya šel ʿAm Yisrael (History of the Jewish People).* II. *The Patriarchs and the Judges.* Tel Aviv, Masada: 1966.
"The World of the Phoenicians," *Natural History* 75 (1966): 14–23.
"Cultural and Religious Life in Canaan in the Days of the New Kingdom." Chapter 4 in vol. 3 of *The World History of the Jewish People.* Ed. B. Mazar. New Brunswick, N.J.: Rutgers University Press, 1971.
"Religion in the World of the Old Testament." Pages 698–73 [Hebrew] in *The President Shazar Festschrift.* Ed. B. Z. Luria. Jerusalem: World Jewish Bible Society, 1973.

"Great Mother of the Gods." Page 700 in Micropaedia vol. 4 of *Encyclopaedia Brittanica*. 15th ed. Chicago, 1974.
"Near Eastern Religions, Ancient." Pages 916–21 in *Encyclopaedia Brittanica*. 15th ed. Chicago, 1974.
"1000 Years Before Abraham," *Midstream* (February 1977): 47–52.
Reply to "The Chaldeans and Haldi," *Biblical Archaeology Review* 3 (4, 1977): 57.
"The Substratum of Taqiyya in Iran," *Journal of the American Oriental Society* 97 (1977): 192.
"1000 Years Before Moses," *Jewish Digest* 24 (2, 1978): 28–34.
"Bronze Age Centers As Philological Centers," *The Ancient World* 2 (2, 1979): 43–45.
"Middle Eastern Religions, Ancient." In *Encyclopaedia Britannica*. 15th ed. Chicago, 1997.

Reviews

Haas, W. S. *Iran*. *Jewish Quarterly Review* 37 (1946): 435–39.
Kramer, S. N. *In the World of Sumer: An Autobiography*. *Journal of Cuneiform Studies* 39 (1987): 247–50.
Malamat, A. *The Arameans in Aram Naharaim and the Rise of Their States*. *Journal of Biblical Literature* 74 (1955): 289.
Muller, H. J. *The Loom of History*. *New York Times Book Review* (1958): 12ff.
Noth, M. *History of Israel*. *Journal of Semitic Studies* 8 (1963): 88–95.
Scharff, A., and A. Moortgat. *Ägypten und Vorderasien im Altertum*. *Orientalia* 21 (1952): 381–83.
Soden, W. von. *Herrscher im alten Orient*. *Orientalia* 25 (1956): 180–81.
Wales, H. G. Q. *The Mountain of God*. *Antiquity* 30 (1956): 232–33.

Aramaic–Syriac–Mandaic Studies

Books

The Living Past. London: Phoenix House, 1941.
Adventures in the Nearest East. London: Phoenix House, 1957.
Opgravingen in Bijbelsegrond. Utrecht: Phoenix House, 1960.

Articles

"An Aramaic Incantation," *Annual of the American Schools of Oriental Research* 14 (1933–1934): 141–44.
"An Aramaic Exorcism," *Archiv Orientální* 6 (1934): 466–74.
"Aramaic Magical Bowls in the Istanbul and Baghdad Museums," *Archiv Orientální* 6 (1934): 319–34.
"The Status of Women Reflected in the Nuzi Tablets," *Zeitschrift für Assyriologie* 43 (1936): 146–69.

"Aramaic and Mandaic Magical Bowls," *Archiv Orientální* 9 (1937): 84–106.
"The Aramaic Incantation in Cuneiform," *Archiv für Orientforschung* 12 (1938): 105–17.
"The Cuneiform Aramaic Incantation," *Orientalia* 9 (1940): 29–38.
"Aramaic Incantation Bowls," *Orientalia* 10 (1941): 116–41, 272–84, 339–60.
"Jam Talism ("A Magic Bowl" in Persian)," *Mehr-e-Iran* (Ordibehesht) (1945 [= 1324]): 7–11.
"A Syriac Incantation," *Bulletin of the American Schools of Oriental Research* 110 (1948): 26–27.
"An Incantation in Estrangelo Script," *Orientalia* 18 (1949): 336–41.
"Two Magic Bowls in Teheran," *Orientalia* 20 (1951): 306–15.
"Aramaic," In *Colliers Encyclopedia*. New York: Colliers, 1952–1953.
"'Holy Waw'? A Case of Contrasting Methodologies," *Orientalia* 22 (1953): 415–16.
"Aramäer." Page 65 in *Religions-Wissenschaftliches Wörterbuch*. Ed. F. König. Freiburg: Herder, 1956.
"Two Aramaic Incantations." Pages 231–44 in *Biblical and Near Eastern Studies: Essays in Honor of William Sanford LaSor*. Ed. G. A. Tuttle. Grand Rapids, Mich.: Eerdmans, 1978.
"The Lance of Qatros," *Aula orientalis* 2 (2, 1984): 80–82.
"Magic Bowls in the Moriah Collection," *Orientalia* 53 (1984): 220–41.
"קתרוס בעל החנית (Qatros of the Lance)," *Bitzaron* 6 NS 24–25 (1984): 53–55.
"The Aramaic Incantation Bowls in Historic Perspective." Pages 142–46 in *Minḥah le-Naḥum: Biblical and Other Studies Presented to Nahum M. Sarna in Honour of his 70th Birthday*. Journal for the Study of the Old Testament: Supplement Series 154. Ed. M. Brettler and M. Fishbane. Sheffield: Sheffield Academic Press, 1993.

Reviews

Drower, E. S. *The Book of the Zodiac*. *Orientalia* 20 (1951) 506–7.
———. *The Coronation of the Great Šišlam*. *Journal of Biblical Literature* 82 (1963): 464.
———. *The Haran Gawaita and the Baptism of Hibil-Ziwa*. *Journal of the Royal Asiatic Society* (1956): 101–2.
———. "The Secret Adam: A Study of Nasoraean Gnosis." *Journal of the Central Conference of American Rabbis* (1961): 69–70.
Dupont-Sommer, A. "A Syrian Incantation." *Bulletin of the American Schools of Oriental Research* 110 (1948): 26–27.
Gignoux, P. *Incantations magiques syriaques*. *Bulletin of the School of Oriental (and African) Studies*.
Krauss, S. *Additamenta ad Librum Aruch Completum*. *Journal of Biblical Literature* 56 (1937): 413–16.

Naveh, J., and S. Shaked. *Amulets and Magic Bowls: Aramaic Incantations of Late Antiquity.* Bulletin of the School of Oriental (and African) Studies 50 (1987): 124.

Rudolph, K. *Mandaeism.* Journal of the American Oriental Society 99 (1979): 476.

Segal, J. B. *The Diacritical Point and the Accents in Syriac.* Orientalia 23 (1954): 329–30.

Sundberg, W. *Kushta: A Monograph on a Principle Word in Mandean Texts.* Orientalia 23 (1954): 205–6.

Art and Archaeology of the Near East

Articles

"Tell Beit Mirsim," *Presbyterian Survey* (1933): 262–65, 325–27, 392–93.

"Buried Treasures of the Near East," *Asia* 36 (1936): 28–33, 120–25.

"Western Asiatic Seals in the Walters Art Gallery," *Iraq* 6 (1939): 3–34.

"Transjordanian Pottery Donated to Smith," *Smith Alumnae Quarterly* (February 1941): 89–90.

"Methods of Biblical Archaeology," *Crozer Quarterly* 27 (1950): 309–12.

"Seals From Ancient Western Asia," *Princeton University Library Chronicle* 12 (2, 1951): 49–55.

"Near Eastern Seals and Cuneiform Tablets," *Princeton University Library Chronicle* 14 (1, 1952): 45–46.

"Near Eastern Seals in Princeton and Philadelphia," *Orientalia* 22 (1953): 242–50.

"Archaeology." Pages 30–31 in *New International 1963 Year Book, Events of 1962.* New York: Funk & Wagnalls, 1963.

"Recovering Canaan and Ancient Israel." Pages 2779–89 in vol. 4 of *Civilizations of the Ancient Near East.* Ed. J. Sasson. 4 vols. New York: Charles Scribner's Sons, 1995.

Reviews

Avi-Yonah, M., and S. Yeivin. *The Antiquities of Israel.* Journal of Near Eastern Studies 17 (1958): 87–88.

Barrois, G. *Manuel d'Archéologie Biblique.* Jewish Quarterly Review 30 (1939): 211–12.

Burrows, M. *What Mean These Stones? The Significance of Archaeology for Biblical Studies.* Jewish Social Studies 4 (1942): 169–70.

Deuel, L. *Testaments of Time: The Search for Lost Manuscripts and Records.* Archaeology (1967): 77–78.

Excavations at Dura–Europos (6th report). Jewish Quarterly Review 28 (1937): 345–46.

Frankfort, H. *Cylinder Seals.* Asia (August 1939): 485.

Glueck, N. *The Other Side of the Jordan.* Jewish Quarterly Review 32 (1941): 413.

———. *Rivers in the Desert: A History of the Negev. Journal of the Central Conference of American Rabbis* (April 1959): 66–67.
Kenyon, F. *The Bible and Archaeology. Jewish Quarterly Review* 32 (1941): 414.
———. *The Bible and Archaeology. Asia* (January 1941): 54–55.
———. *Royal Cities of the Old Testament. American Historical Review* (1975): 76–77.
Mindlin, M., et al. *Figurative Language in the Ancient Near East. Bulletin of the School of Oriental (and African) Studies* 53 (1989): 122–23.
Mallowan, M. *Early Mesopotamia and Iran. Journal of Semitic Studies* 12 (1967): 109.
———. *Nimrud and Its Remains. Natural History* 75 (1966): 68–70.
Morris, Y. *Masters of the Desert: 6000 Years in the Negev. Saturday Review* (1961): 30–31.
Phillips, W. *Qataban and Sheba. Antiquity* 30 (1956): 60–61.
Speiser, E. *Excavations at Tepe Gawra*, vol. I. *Asia* (January 1936): 67–68.

Assyriology

Books

Smith College Tablets: 110 Cuneiform Texts Selected From the College Collection. Northampton, Mass.: Dept. of History of Smith College, 1952.
Hammurapi's Code: Quaint or Forward Looking? New York: Rinehart, 1957.

Articles

"Eight New Cuneiform Fragments From Tell El Amarna," *Journal of Egyptian Archaeology* 20 (3–4, 1934): 137–38.
"The New Amarna Tablets," *Orientalia* 16 (1947): 1–21.
"Šamši-Adad's Military Texts From Mari," *Archiv Orientální* 18 (1950): 199–207.
"Damascus in Assyrian Sources," *Israel Exploration Journal* 2 (1952): 174–75.
Introduction to *A Cylinder of Nebuchadrezzar II,* by E. B. Smick. Ringwood, N.J.: Department of Semitics of Shelton College, 1953.
"Stratification of Society in Hammurapi's Code." Pages 17–28 in *The Joshua Starr Memorial Volume.* Jewish Social Studies 5. Ed. A. Duker et al. New York: Conference of Jewish Relations, 1953.
"Observations on the Akkadian Tablets From Ugarit," *Revue d'assyriologie et d'archéologie orientale* 50 (1956): 127–33.
"Babylonia." In *The New Book of Knowledge.* Danbury, Conn.: Grolier's, 1966.
"Origins of the Gilgamesh Epic." Introduction to *He Who Saw Everything,* by Anita Feagle. New York: Young Scott Books, 1966.
"Vocalized Consonants: The Key to *um-ma / en-ma /* נאם." Pages 109–10 in *The Tablet and the Scroll: Near Eastern Studies in Honor of William*

W. Hallo. Ed. M. E. Cohen, D. C. Snell, and D. B. Weisberg. Bethesda, Md.: CDL Press, 1993.

"The Gilgamesh Epic." Page 254 in *Oxford Companion to the Bible*. Ed. B. Metzger and M. Coogan. New York: Oxford University Press, 1993.

Collaborative Works

Pohl, A., and C. H. Gordon. "Keilschriftbibliographie 2," *Orientalia* 10 (1941): 93–103.

———. "Keilschriftbibliographie 3," *Orientalia* 10 (1941): 241–53.

———. "Keilschriftbibliographie 4," *Orientalia* 11 (1942): 134–47.

———. "Keilschriftbibliographie 5," *Orientalia* 12 (1943): 91–109.

———. "Keilschriftbibliographie 9," *Orientalia* 16 (1947): 85–102.

———. "Keilschriftbibliographie 10," *Orientalia* 16 (1947): 491–505.

Reviews

Böhl, M. *Akkadian Chrestomathy I: Selected Cuneiform Texts*. *Orientalia* 19 (1950): 479–80.

Ebeling, E. *Bruchstücke einer mittelassyrischen Vorschriftensammlung von Wagenpferden*. *Orientalia* 22 (1953): 231–32.

Heidel, A. *The Gilgamesh Epic and Old Testament Parallels*. *American Journal of Archaeology* 54 (1950): 148–49.

Mercer, S. A. B. *The Tell El-Amarna Tablets*. *University of Toronto Quarterly* 9 (1940): 242–44.

Parker, R. A., and W. H. Dubberstein. *Babylonian Chronology, 626 B.C–A.D. 45*. *American Historical Review* (1943): 140.

Rutten, M. *Éléments d'Accadien*. *Jewish Quarterly Review* 30 (1939): 212–15.

Soden, W. von. *Das Akkadische Syllabar*. Analecta orientalia 27. *Orientalia* 19 (1950): 90–93.

———. *Grundriss der akkadischen Grammatik*. Analecta orientalia 33. *Orientalia* 22 (1953): 227–31.

Ungnad, A. *Grammatik des Akkadischen*. *Orientalia* 19 (1950): 88–90.

Biblical Studies

Book

New Horizons in Old Testament Literature. Ventnor, N.J.: Ventnor Publishers, 1960.

Articles

"Rabbinic Exegesis in the Vulgate of Proverbs," *Journal of Biblical Literature* 49 (1930): 384–416.

"Fratriarchy in the Old Testament," *Journal of Biblical Literature* 54 (1935): 223–31.

"A New Akkadian Parallel to Deuteronomy 25:11–12," *Journal of the Palestine Oriental Society* 15 (1935): 29–34.

"אלהים in Its Reputed Meaning of 'Rulers, Judges'," *Journal of Biblical Literature* 54 (1935): 139–44.

"An Akkadian Parallel to Deuteronomy 21:1ff," *Revue d'Assyriologie* 33 (1936): 1–6.

"Hosea 2:4–5 in the Light of New Semitic Inscriptions," *Zeitschrift für die alttestamentliche Wissenschaft* 54 (1936): 277–80.

"חֻקֵּי הַתּוֹרָה וְלוּחוֹת אַשּׁוּר," *Hadoar* 39 (1936; 28 Tishre 5696): 747–48.

"The Story of Jacob and Laban in the Light of the Nuzi Tablets," *Bulletin of the American Schools of Oriental Research* 66 (1937): 25–27.

"Zu ZAW 1936," *Zeitschrift für die alttestamentliche Wissenschaft* 55 (1937): 176.

"The Pointing of יהוה," *Zeitschrift für die alttestamentliche Wissenschaft* 15 (1938): 174.

"Biblical Customs and the Nuzu Tablets," *Biblical Archaeologist* 3 (1940): 1–12.

"סִפּוּרֵי הַמִּקְרָא לְאוֹר הַחֲפִירוֹת (Biblical Narratives in the Light of Archaeology)," *Bitzaron* 3 (1940): 162–71.

"A Daniel Come to Judgment," *The Shakespeare Association Bulletin* 15 (1940): 206–9.

"New Light on the Old Testament," *The Bible Today* 42 (4, 1949): 131–35.

"Belt-Wrestling in the Bible World," *Hebrew Union College Annual* 23 (1950): 131–36.

"Into All Truth: John 16:13," *Discovery* 2 (2, 1950): 16–22.

"Masorah." In *Colliers Encyclopedia*. New York: Colliers, 1952–1953.

"ᶜAlmah in Isaiah 7:14," *Journal of Bible and Religion* 21 (1953): 106.

"The Patriarchal Age," *Journal of Bible and Religion* 21 (1953): 238–43.

"The Patriarchal Narratives," *Journal of Near Eastern Studies* 13 (1954): 56–59.

"Abraham and the Merchants of Ura," *Journal of Near Eastern Studies* 17 (1958): 28–31.

"Kanaanäer." Pages 440–41 in *Religions-Wissenschaftliches Wörterbuch*. Ed. F. König. Freiburg: Herder, 1956.

"Semiten." Pages 813–16 in *Religions-Wissenschaftliches Wörterbuch*. Ed. F. König. Freiburg: Herder, 1956.

"Indo–European and Hebrew Epic," *Eretz-Israel* (Benjamin Mazar Festschrift) 5 (1958): 10–15.

"Higher Critics and Forbidden Fruit," *Christianity Today* 4 (November 23, 1959): 3–6.

"David the Dancer." Pages 46–49 in *Yehezkel Kaufman Jubilee Volume*. Ed. M. Haran. Jerusalem: Magnes, 1960.

"The Bible in New Perspective," *American Judaism* 11 (Winter, 1961): 6–17.

"Accad," "Ahava," "Aram-Naharaim," "Arpachshad," "Asshur," "Beth–Eden," "Calah," "Calneh," "Carchemish," "Diphath," "Dodanim," "Gozan,"

"Habor," "Halah," "Haran," "Kir," "Mesopotamia," "Mitanni," "Paddan-Aram," Riphath," "Rodanim," "Tarshish," "Tel-Assar," "Teraphim," "Tiras," "Wrestling." In *The Interpreter's Dictionary of the Bible*. Ed. G. A. Buttrick. 4 vols. New York: Abingdon Press, 1962.

"Genesis and Archaeological Discovery," *The Jewish Teacher* 29 (April 1962): 7–10.

"Abraham of Ur." Pages 77–84 in *Hebrew and Semitic Studies*. Ed. D. W. Thomas and W. D. McHardy. Oxford: Clarendon, 1963.

"Hebrew Origins in the Light of Recent Discoveries." Pages 3–14 in *Biblical and Other Studies*. Lown Institute Studies 1. Ed. A. Altman. Cambridge, Mass.: Harvard University Press, 1963.

"A Note on the Tenth Commandment," *Journal of Bible and Religion* 31 (1963): 2–8, 209.

"Re: *Before the Bible*," *New Statesman* (1963): 271.

"Hebrew Origins," *Jewish Heritage* (1964): 12–50.

"The Ten Commandments." *Christianity Today* 8 (April 10, 1964): 625–28.

"Abraham the Basileus," *Jahrbuch für Kleinasiatische Forschung (Anadolu Arastirmalari)* (Bossert Memorial Volume) 2 (1965): 227–30.

"The Apocrypha." Pages 156–59 in *The New Book of Knowledge*. Danbury, Conn.: Grolier, 1966.

"The Background and Character of Biblical Israel," *Perspectives in Jewish Learning* 2 (1966): 1–16.

"Higher Critics and Forbidden Fruit." Pages 67–73 in *A Christianity Today Reader*. New York: Meredith Press, 1966. Repr. of *Christianity Today* 4 (November 23, 1959): 3–6.

"Leviathan: Symbol of Evil." Pages 1–9 in *Biblical Motifs*. Ed. A. Altman. Cambridge. Harvard University Press, 1966.

"Temple of Solomon." In *Encyclopaedia Brittanica*. 14th ed. Chicago, 1967.

"His Name is 'One'," *Journal of Near Eastern Studies* 29 (1970): 198–99.

"The New English Bible, Old Testament," *Christianity Today* (March 17, 1970): 574–76.

"Riddles of the Wise," *Berytus* 21 (1972): 17–33.

"He Is Who He Is," *Berytus* 23 (1974): 27–28.

"Solomon." Pages 1044–45 in *Encyclopaedia Brittanica*. Chicago, 1974.

"Does the Gospel of Matthew Proclaim Mary's Virginity?" *Biblical Archaeological Review* 3 (3, 1977): 53.

"Paternity at Two Levels," *Journal of Biblical Literature* 96 (1977): 101.

"Reflections on Hebrew Origins," *Midstream* (October 1977): 41–46.

"Where Is Abraham's Ur?" *Biblical Archaeological Review* 3 (2, 1977): 20–21, 52.

"Build-Up and Climax." Pages 29–34 in *Studies in Bible and the Ancient Near East Presented to Samuel E. Loewenstamm*. Jerusalem: E. Rubenstein, 1978.

"The Double Paternity of Jesus," *Biblical Archaeological Review* 4 (2, 1978): 26–27.

"History of Religion in Psalm 82." Pages 129–31 in *Biblical and Near Eastern Studies: Essays in Honor of William Sanford LaSor*. Ed. G. A. Tuttle. Grand Rapids, Mich.: Eerdmans, 1978.

Replies to "Queries and Comments," *Biblical Archaeological Review* 4 (3, 1978): 45–47.

"The Wine-Dark Sea," *Journal of Near Eastern Studies* 37 (1978): 51–52.

"The Background of David's Achievements," *Midstream* 25 (2, 1979): 43–48.

"היום השביעי (The Seventh Day)" *Bitzaron* 1 NS 1–2 (1979): 20–22.

"Ancient Israel and Egypt," *New York University Education Quarterly* 12 (4, 1981): 9–13.

"'In' of Predication or Equivalence," *Journal of Biblical Literature* 100 (1981): 612–13.

"Asymmetric Janus Parallelism," *Eretz-Israel: Archaeological, Historical and Geographical Studies* 16 (1982): 80–81.

"The Biblical Sabbath: Its Origin and Observance in the Ancient Near East," *Judaism* 31 (1982): 12–16.

"Ebla and Genesis 11." Pages 125–34 in *A Spectrum of Thought: Essays in Honor of Dennis F. Kinlaw*. Ed. M. L. Peterson. Wilmore, Ky.: Asbury College Press, 1982.

"The International God Elohim/Ntr," *Hebrew Studies* 23 (1982): 33–35.

"Khnum and El," *Egyptological Studies* 28 (1982): 203–13.

"Jewish Reactions to Christian Borrowings." Pages 685–90 in *The Word of the Lord Shall Go Forth*. D.N. Freedman Festschrift. Winona Lake, Ind.: Eisenbrauns, 1983.

"A Scholar and Gentleman: James Alan Montgomery," *Biblical Archaeologist* 46 (1983): 187–89.

"דרכי הסתיינות היהדות מן הנצרות (Jewish Reactions to Christian Borrowings)," *Bitzaron* 5 NS 17–18 (1983): 78–80.

"War and Peace: The Theoretical Structure of Israelite Society." Pages 299–303 in *Fields of Offerings*. Raphael Patai Festschrift. Ed. V. D. Sanua. Farleigh Dickinson University Press, 1983.

"Max L. Margolis," *Academic Life at New York University* 3 (5, 1984).

"On Making Other Gods." Pages 77–79 in *Biblical and Related Studies Presented to Samuel Iwry*. Ed. A. Kort and S. Morschauser. Winona Lake, Ind.: Eisenbrauns, 1985.

"The International God Elohim/Ntr." Pages 181–85 in *A Companion to the Bible*. Ed. R. S. M. Miriam Ward. New York: Alba House, 1985. Repr. of *Hebrew Studies* 23 (1982): 33–35.

"The Marriage and Death of Sinuhe." Pages 43–44 in *Love and Death in the Ancient Near East: Essays in Honor of Marvin H. Pope*. Ed. J. H. Marks and R. M. Good. Guilford, Conn.: Four Quarters, 1987.

"Ugaritic RBT / RABITU." Pages 127–32 in *Ascribe to the Lord: Biblical and Other Studies in Memory of Peter C. Craigie*. Ed. L. Eslinger and G. Taylor. Journal for the Study of the Old Testament: Supplement Series 67. Sheffield: Sheffield Academic Press, 1988.

"Ebla, Ugarit and the Old Testament," *Orient* 25 (1989): 134–68.

"'This Time' (Genesis 2:23)." Pages 47–51 in *Sha'arei Talmon: Studies in the Bible, Qumran, and the Ancient Near East Presented to Shemaryahu Talmon*. Ed. M. Fishbane and E. Tov. Winona Lake, Ind.: Eisenbrauns, 1992.

"The Background to Jewish Studies in the Bible and in the Ancient East," *Shofar* 12 (4, 1994): 1–46.

"James Alan Montgomery." In *American National Biography*. Ed. J. Garraty. Cary, N.C.: Oxford University Press, 1994.

"Recovering Canaan and Ancient Israel." Pages 2779–89 in vol. 4 of *Civilizations of the Ancient Near East*. Ed. J. Sasson. 4 vols. New York: Charles Scribner's Sons, 1995.

"Mesopotamia: Land of Myths." Pages 22–27 in *Genesis: World of Myths*. Ed. A. Feyerick. New York: New York University Press, 1996.

"Canaan: Land Between Empires." Pages 84–87 in *Genesis: World of Myths*. Ed. A. Feyerick. New York: New York University Press, 1996.

"Egypt: The Nurturing Land." Pages 168–73 in *Genesis: World of Myths*. Ed. A. Feyerick. New York: New York University Press, 1996.

"The Background of Some Distinctive Values in the Hebrew Bible." Pages 57–68 in *Go to the Land I Will Show You: Studies in Honor of Dwight W. Young*. Ed. J. E. Coleson and V. H. Matthews. Winona Lake, Ind.: Eisenbrauns, 1996.

Reviews

Burrows, M. *What Mean These Stones? The Significance of Archaeology for Biblical Studies*. Jewish Social Studies 4 (1942): 169–70.

Garstang, J., and J. B. E. Garstang. *The Story of Jericho*. Jewish Quarterly Review 31 (1941): 414.

Grollenberg, L. H. *Atlas of the Bible*. Jewish Social Studies 19 (1957): 146.

Hebrew Union College Annual 19. Journal of Biblical Literature 66 (1947): 247.

Kusch, H., ed. *Festschrift Franz Dornseiff (zum 65 Geburtstag)*. 1953.

Neufeld, E. *Ancient Hebrew Marriage Laws*. Jewish Quarterly Review 40 (1949–1950): 125.

Orlinsky, H. *Ancient Israel*. Journal of the American Oriental Society 74 (1954): 268.

Pope, M. H. *Song of Songs: A New Translation With Introduction and Commentary*. Anchor Bible. Journal of the American Oriental Society 100 (1980): 354–57.

Schmidt, J. *Studien zur Stilistik des alttestamentlichen Spruchliteratur. Journal of Biblical Literature* 56 (1937): 137.
The Torah: The Five Books of Moses. (A new translation of the Holy Scriptures; Jewish Publication Society of America) *Saturday Review* (May 11, 1963): 76.
Tournay, R. J. *Quand Dieu parle aux hommes le langage d'amour: Études sur Le Cantique des Cantiques. Journal of the American Oriental Society* 104 (1984): 766–67.

Comparative Literature and Linguistics

Books

Before the Bible: The Common Background of Greek and Hebrew Civilization. New York: Harper and Row, 1962.
Före Bibeln och Homeros. Stockholm: Bonniers, 1964. Swedish trans. of *Before the Bible.*
The Common Background of Greek and Hebrew Civilization. New York: W. W. Norton, 1965. Rev. ed. of *Before the Bible.*
לפני היות התנ"ך. Tel Aviv: Am Oved and Devir Presses, 1966. Hebrew trans. of *Before the Bible.*
Ugarit and Minoan Crete. New York: W. W. Norton, 1966.
Voor de Bijbel. Utrecht: Aula-Boeken, 1966. Dutch trans. of *Before the Bible.*
Homer and Bible: The Origin and Character of East Mediterranean Literature. Ventnor, N.J.: Ventnor Publishers, 1967.
Seisho-izen. Tokyo: Misuzu Shobo, 1967. Japanese trans. of *Before the Bible.*
Before the Bible. Plainview, N.Y.: Books for Libraries, 1973.

Articles

"Ugarit As Link Between Greek and Hebrew Literatures," *Revista degli studi orientali* 29 (1954): 161–69.
"Homer and Bible: The Origin and Character of Mediterranean Literature," *Hebrew Union College Annual* 26 (1955): 43–108.
"Homer, Caphtor and Canaan," *Anadolu Arastirmalari* 1 (1955): 139–46.
"Un ceppo comune della cultura greca ed ebraica," *Voice of America* broadcast (March 23, 1956).
"The Common Background of Hebrew and Greek Civilization," *Graduate Comment* (Wayne State University) 7 (1, 1963): 1–4, 12.
"Concerning *Before the Bible*," *New Statesman* (February 22, 1963): 271.
"The Mediterranean Factor in the Old Testament." Pages 19–31 in *Congress Volume, Bonn 1962.* Supplements to Vetus Testamentum 9. Leiden: E. J. Brill, 1963.
"Comment by Professor Cyrus H. Gordon (in responce to article by Jan Dus)," *Jewish Social Studies* 10 (1965): 57–58.

"The Greeks and the Hebrews," *Scientific American* 212 (February 1965): 102–11.

"Re: 'The Greeks and the Hebrews'," *Scientific American* 212 (August 1965): 6.

"Griegos y hebreos," *Revista de Occidents* 4 (43, 1966): 43–61. Spanish trans. of "The Greeks and the Hebrews," *Scientific American* 212 (February 1965): 102–11.

"Hebrews and Greeks," *Hadassah Magazine* 48 (1966): 3–4.

"Hellenes and Hebrews," *Greek Orthodox Theological Review* 12 (1967): 134–40.

"Links Between Ancient Greeks and Hebrews," *The Jewish Digest* 12 (September 1967): 37–40.

"Vergil and the Near East," *Ugaritica, Dedicated to C. Schaeffer* 6 (1969): 267–88.

"A Tragic Discrepancy Between Roman and Semitic Law," *Manuscripts* 22 (1970): 34–35.

"Vergil and the Bible World." Pages 111–30 in *Gratz College Anniversary Volume*. Ed. A. Neuman. Philadelphia: Jewish Publication Society, 1971.

"Ugarit and Its Significance to Biblical Studies." In *Biblical Studies in Contemporary Thought*. Ed. M. Ward. Burlington, Vt.: Trinity College Biblical Institute, 1975.

"The Greeks and the Hebrews," *Dokkyo University Bulletin of Liberal Arts* 11 (December 1976): 25–44.

"New Directions," *The Bulletin of the American Society of Papyrologists (Studies Presented to Naphtali Lewis)* 15 (1978): 1–2, 59–66.

"Recovering Canaan and Ancient Israel." Pages 2779–89 in vol. 4 of *Civilizations of the Ancient Near East*. Ed. J. Sasson. 4 vols. New York: Charles Scribner's Sons, 1995.

"Father's Sons and Mother's Daughters: The Problem of Indo-European–Semitic Relationships." Pages 271–78 in *Crossing Boundaries and Linking Horizons: Studies in Honor of Michael C. Astour on His 80th Birthday*. Ed. G. D. Young, M. W. Chavalas, and R. E. Averbeck. Bethesda, Md.: CDL Press, 1997.

"The Common Background of Greek and Hebrew Civilization. Pages 1–5 in *Hellenic and Jewish Arts*. Ed. A. Ovadiah. Tel Aviv: Tel Aviv University, 1998.

Reviews

Cross, F. M. *Canaanite Myth and Hebrew Epic: Essays in the History of the Religion of Israel*. *American Historical Review* 79 (1974): 1149.

Levin, S. *The Indo-European and Semitic Languages*. *Journal of the American Academy of Religion, Supplement* (1975): 313–14.

Masson, E. *Recherches sur les plus anciens emprunts sémitiques en Grec*. Études et Commentairies 67. *Journal of Hellenic Studies* "Notice of Books" (1968): 188–89.

Pritchard, J. B. *Ancient Near Eastern Texts Relating to the Old Testament. American Journal of Archaeology* 56 (1952): 93–94.

Rosenman, J. *Primitive Speech and English. Journal of Near Eastern Studies* 31 (1972): 234–35.

Velikovsky, I. *Oedipus and Akhnaton. Pensée* (1972): 30–32.

Current Affairs

Book

Lands of the Cross and Crescent. Ventnor, N.J.: Ventnor Publishers, 1948.

Articles

"Satan's Worshippers in Kurdistan," *Asia* 35 (1935): 625–30.
"Our Homes are Thine," *Asia* 37 (1937): 559–62.
"'Club Life' in Transjordania," *Jewish Outlook* (June 1938): 9–12.
"The Problem of Israel," *Current History* (June 1956): 347–52.
"Albania." In *Colliers Encyclopedia Yearbook 1961.* New York: Colliers, 1962.
"Cyprus." In *Colliers Encyclopedia Yearbook 1961.* New York: Colliers, 1962.
"Greece." In *Colliers Encyclopedia Yearbook 1961.* New York: Colliers, 1962.
"The Humanities and Our Future," *Mount Vernon Alumnae Bulletin* (Spring 1968): 36–37.
"Should Israel Be a Pluralist State?" *The Boston Globe* (February 9, 1976): 15.

Dead Sea Scrolls

Articles

"The Dead Sea Scrolls," *The Reconstructionist* 22 (6, 1956): 8–15.
"Selected Books on the Dead Sea Scrolls." Pages 12–18 in *Jewish Book Annual* 17. Ed. A. Steinbach. New York: Marstin Press, 1959.

Review

Barthélemy, D., and J. T. Milik. *Qumran Cave I. Antiquity* 30 (1956): 118.

Ebla

Articles

"Ebla and the Minoan Problem." Pages 209–12 in vol. 1 of *Studia Mediterranea: Piero Meriggi dicata.* Ed. O. Carruba. Pavia, 1979.
"Eblaite and Its Affinities." Pages 297–301 in *Amsterdam Studies in the Theory and History of Linguistic Science. IV. Current Issues in Linguistic Theory.* Oswald Szemerényi Festschrift. Amsterdam: John Benjamins, 1979.

"Echoes of Ebla." Pages 133–39 in *Essays on the Occasion of the Seventieth Anniversary of The Dropsie University*. Philadelphia, Penn.: Dropsie University Press, 1979.

"The Seventh Day," *Ugarit-Forschungen* 11 (1979): 299–301.

"לוחות אבלה ועולם המקרא (The Ebla Tablets and the Biblical World)," *Hebrew Studies* 22 (1981): 39–47.

"Ebla and Genesis 11." Pages 125–34 in *A Spectrum of Thought: Essays in Honor of Dennis F. Kinlaw*. Ed. M. L. Peterson. Wilmore, Ky.: Asbury College Press, 1982.

"The 'Waw Conversive': From Eblaite to Hebrew," *The American Academy for Jewish Research* 50 (1983): 87–90.

"The Ugaritic Texts: Half a Century of Research." Pages 492–501 in *Biblical Archaeology Today: Proceedings of the International Congress on Biblical Archaeology*. Ed. J. Amitai. Jerusalem: Israel Exploration Society; The Israel Academy of Sciences and Humanities, in cooperation with American Schools of Oriental Research, 1985.

"ḤBY, Possessor of Horns and Tail," *Ugarit-Forschungen* 18 (1986): 129–32.

Introduction (pp. 1–5) to vol. 1 of *Eblaitica: Essays on the Ebla Archives and the Eblaite Language*. Ed. C. H. Gordon, G. A. Rendsburg, and N. H. Winter. Winona Lake, Ind.: Eisenbrauns, 1987.

"Eblaitica." Pages 19–28 in vol. 1 of *Eblaitica: Essays on the Ebla Archives and the Eblaite Language*. Ed. C. H. Gordon, G. A. Rendsburg, and N. H. Winter. Winona Lake, Ind.: Eisenbrauns, 1987.

"Personal Names of the 'Verb + Deity' Type From Ebla." *Rencontre Assyriologique Internationale*. Istanbul, 1987.

"WM– 'and' in Eblaite and Hebrew." Pages 29–41 in vol. 1 of *Eblaitica: Essays on the Ebla Archives and the Eblaite Language*. Ed. C. H. Gordon, G. A. Rendsburg, and N. H. Winter. Winona Lake, Ind.: Eisenbrauns, 1987.

"Ebla As Background for the Old Testament." Pages 293–97 in *Congress Volume, Jerusalem 1986*. Supplements to Vetus Testamentum 40. Leiden: E. J. Brill, 1988.

"Notes on Proper Names in the Ebla Tablets." Pages 153–58 in vol. 1 of *Archivi Reali di Ebla-Studi*. Ed. A. Archi. Rome, 1988.

"West Semitic Factors in Eblaite." Pages 261–66 in *Current Issues in Linguistic Theory: FUCUS: A Semitic/Afrasian Gathering in Remembrance of Albert Ehrman*. Ed. Yoël L. Arbeitman. Amsterdam: John Benjamins, 1988.

"Ebla, Ugarit and the Old Testament," *Orient* 25 (1989): 134–68.

"Ebla and the Old Testament (in Korean)." 1990.

"Eblaite and Northwest Semitic." Pages 127–39 in vol. 2 of *Eblaitica: Essays on the Ebla Archives and the Eblaite Language*. Ed. C. H. Gordon and G. A. Rendsburg. Winona Lake, Ind.: Eisenbrauns, 1990.

"In Memoriam: Claude Frederic Armand Schaeffer (1898–1982)." Pages 127–30 in vol. 2 of *Eblaitica: Essays on the Ebla Archives and the Eblaite Language*. Ed. C. H. Gordon and G. A. Rendsburg. Winona Lake, Ind.: Eisenbrauns, 1990.
Introduction (p. 1) to vol. 2 of *Eblaitica: Essays on the Ebla Archives and the Eblaite Language*. Ed. C. H. Gordon and G. A. Rendsburg. Winona Lake, Ind.: Eisenbrauns, 1990.
"A Response to W. G. Lambert." Pages 145–46 in vol. 2 of *Eblaitica: Essays on the Ebla Archives and the Eblaite Language*. Ed. C. H. Gordon and G. A. Rendsburg. Winona Lake, Ind.: Eisenbrauns, 1990.
"The Ebla Incantations and Their Affinities With Northwest Semitic Magic," *Maarav* (Stanley Gewirtz Festschrift) 7 (1991): 117–29.
"Eblaite." Pages 550–57 in *Semitic Studies: In Honor of Wolf Leslau, On the Occasion of His Eighty-Fifth Birthday November 14th, 1991*. Ed. A. S. Kaye. Wiesbaden: Otto Harrossowitz, 1991.
Introduction (p. 1) to vol. 3 of *Eblaitica: Essays on the Ebla Archives and the Eblaite Language*. Ed. C. H. Gordon and G. A. Rendsburg. Winona Lake, Ind.: Eisenbrauns, 1992.
"The Ebla Exorcisms." Pages 127–37 in vol. 3 of *Eblaitica: Essays on the Ebla Archives and the Eblaite Language*. Ed. C. H. Gordon and G. A. Rendsburg. Winona Lake, Ind.: Eisenbrauns, 1992.
"The Eblaite Language." Pages 101–7 in *Contacts Between Cultures*. Ed. A. Harrak. Lewiston, N.Y.: Edwin Mellen, 1992.
"The Geographical Horizons of Ebla," *Bibliotheca Mesopotamica* 25 (1992): 63–68.
"Vocalized Consonants: The Key to *um–ma* / *en–ma* / נְאֻם." Pages 109–10 in *The Tablet and the Scroll: Near Eastern Studies in Honor of William W. Hallo*. Ed. M. E. Cohen, D. C. Snell, and D. B. Weisberg. Bethesda, Md.: CDL Press, 1993.
"Ebla." Page 176 in *Oxford Companion to the Bible*. Ed. B. Metzger and M. Coogan. New York: Oxford University Press, 1993.
"Ebla." Pages 500–501 in *Colliers Encyclopedia*. New York: Colliers, 1995.
"Eblaite Phonology." In *Phonologies of Asia and Africa (Including the Caucasus)*. Ed. Alan S. Kaye. Winona Lake, Ind.: Eisenbrauns, 1997.

Egypto-Semitic Studies

Articles

"The Feminine Singulars of the Egyptian Demonstrative Pronouns," *Journal of the American Oriental Society* 49 (1929): 58–60.
"Marginal Notes on the Ancient Middle East," *Jahrbuch für kleinasiatische Forschung* 2 (August 1951): 50–62.

"Egypto-Semitica." Pages 269–77 in *Scritti in onore di Giuseppe Furlani*. Ed. G. Bardi. = *Revista degli studi orientali* 32 (1957).

"Ancient Letters to the Dead and Others," *Natural History* 78 (February 1969): 94–99.

"Egypto-Semitic Magic Bowls." Pages 165–73 in vol. 1 of *Hagut Ivrit b-Amerika*. Ed. M. Zohari, A. Tartakover, and H. Ormian. Tel Aviv: Yavneh, 1972.

"'In' of Predication or Equivalence," *Journal of Biblical Literature* 100 (1981): 612–13.

"The International God Elohim/Ntr," *Hebrew Studies* 23 (1982): 33–35.

"Khnum and El," *Egyptological Studies* 28 (1982): 203–13.

"The International God Elohim/Ntr." Pages 181–85 in *A Companion to the Bible*. Ed. R. S. M. Miriam Ward. New York: Alba House, 1985. Repr. of *Hebrew Studies* 23 (1982): 33–35.

"The Marriage and Death of Sinuhe." Pages 43–44 in *Love and Death in the Ancient Near East: Essays in Honor of Marvin H. Pope*. Ed. J. H. Marks and R. M. Good. Guilford, Conn.: Four Quarters, 1987.

"New Directions in the Study of Ancient Middle Eastern Cultures." Pages 53–65 in *Bulletin of the Middle Eastern Culture Center in Japan. V. Near Eastern Studies: Dedicated to H. I. H. Prince Takahito Mikasa on the Occasion of His Seventy-Fifth Birthday*. Ed. M. Mori. Wiesbaden: Otto Harrassowitz, 1991.

Reviews

Golomb, D. M., and S. T. Hollis. *"Working with No Data": Semitic and Egyptian Studies Presented to Thomas O. Lambdin*. *Bulletin of the School of Oriental (and African) Studies* 53 (1990): 124–25.

Hoch, J. E. *Semitic Words in Egyptian Texts of the New Kingdon and Intermediate Period*. *Catholic Biblical Quarterly* 57 (1995): 770–71.

Steindorff, G. *Lehrbuch der koptischen Grammatik*. *Journal of Biblical Literature* 75 (1956): 61–62.

General Semitic Studies

Book

The Pennsylvania Tradition of Semitics. Society of Biblical Literature Centennial Publications. Atlanta: Scholars Press, 1986.

Articles

"Semitic Languages and Literatures." Pages 862–64 in *The American Yearbook: A Record of Events and Progress 1937*. New York: Thomas Nelson, 1938.

"Semitic Languages and Literatures." Pages 850–52 in *The American Yearbook: A Record of Events and Progress 1938*. New York: Thomas Nelson, 1939.

"Semitic Languages and Literatures." Pages 889–91 in *The American Yearbook: A Record of Events and Progress 1939.* New York: Thomas Nelson, 1940.

Reviews

Rinaldi, G. *Le lingue semitische: Introduzione generale storica e bibliographica.* Catholic Biblical Quarterly 17 (1955): 621–22.

Speiser, E. *Introduction to Hurrian.* Annual of the American Schools of Oriental Research 20. *American Journal of Archaeology* 46 (1942).

Hebrew Language

Articles

"The Accentual Shift in the Perfect With the Waw Consecutive," *Journal of Biblical Literature* 57 (1938): 319–25.

"The Relationship Between Modern and Biblical Hebrew," First Annual Meeting of the National Association of Hebrew Professors, New York City, 1951.

"Hebrew." In *Colliers Encyclopedia.* New York: Colliers, 1952–1953.

"השפעה צפון־ישראלית על העברית שלאחר־גלות בבל," *Eretz-Israel (Dedicated to the Memory of M. D. U. Cassuto)* 3 (1954): 104–5.

"North Israelite Influence on Postexilic Hebrew," *Israel Exploration Journal* 5 (1955): 85–88.

"חודש (Month)." Pages 36–40 in vol. 3 of ג אנציקלופדיה מקראית *Biblical Encyclopedia,* 1958.

"Hebrew אחדים = ILTÊNÛTU 'Pair'." Pages 5–9 in *Sepher Segal.* Jerusalem: The Israel Society for Biblical Research, 1965.

"The Language of Crete: A New Area for the Science of the Hebrew Language." Pages 186–239 in vol. 1 of *Hagut Ivrit b-Amerika.* Ed. M. Zohari, A. Tartakover, and H. Ormian. Tel Aviv: Yavneh, 1972.

"New Light on the Hebrew Language," *Hebrew Abstracts, The David Rudavsky Issue* 15 (1974): 29–31.

"Hebrew Language." Pages 392–94 in *Interpreter's Dictionary of the Bible: Supplementary Volume.* Ed. K. Crim. Nashville, Abingdon: 1976.

"Extensions of Barth's Law of Vocalic Sequence," *Orientalia* 51 (1982): 394–96.

"The 'Waw Conversive': From Eblaite to Hebrew." *The American Academy for Jewish Research* 50 (1983): 87–90.

"WM– 'and' in Eblaite and Hebrew." Pages 29–41 in vol. 1 of *Eblaitica: Essays on the Ebla Archives and the Eblaite Language.* Ed. C. H. Gordon, G. A. Rendsburg, and N. H. Winter. Winona Lake, Ind.: Eisenbrauns, 1987.

"Vocalized Consonants: The Key to *um–ma / en–ma /* נְאֻם." Pages 109–10 in *The Tablet and the Scroll: Near Eastern Studies in Honor of William W. Hallo.* Ed. M. E. Cohen, D. C. Snell, and D. B. Weisberg. Bethesda, Md.: CDL Press, 1993.

Review

Cross, F. M., and D. N. Freedman. *Early Hebrew Orthography: A Study of the Epigraphic Evidence.* Orientalia 23 (1954): 206.

Judaic Miscellanea

Article

"The Origin of the Jews in Elephantine," *Journal of Near Eastern Studies* 14 (1955): 56–58.

Reviews

Cavalletti, S. *Il Trattato delle Benedizioni (Berakhot) del Talmud Babilonese.* Catholic Biblical Quarterly 31 (1969): 418–19.
Eddy, S. K. *The King is Dead: Studies in the Near Eastern Resistance to Hellenism (334–31 B.C.).* American Historical Review 69 (1964): 497.
Gordis, R. *Max Margolis: Scholar and Teacher.* Jewish Social Studies 17 (1955): 163.
Koestler, A. *The Thirteenth Tribe.* Boston Sunday Herald Advertiser (September 26, 1976): Section 6, page A15.
Leslau, W. *Falasha Anthology.* Crozer Quarterly 29 (1952): 249–50.
Mazar, B. *The World History of the Jewish People,* vol. 2. American Historical Review 78 (1973): 411–13.
Porten, B. *Archives From Elephantine: The Life of an Ancient Jewish Military Colony.* American Historical Review 75 (1969): 88–89.
Schalit, A. *The World History of the Jewish People,* vol. 6. American Historical Review 79 (1974): 489.

Long-Range Diffusion

Books

Before Columbus: Links Between the Old World and Ancient America. New York: Crown Publishers, 1971.
Riddles in History. New York: Crown Publishers, 1974.

Articles

"The Authenticity of the Phoenician Text From Parahyba," *Orientalia* 37 (1968): 75–80.
"The Canaanite Text From Brazil," *Orientalia* 37 (1968): 425–36.
"Canaan e a América Pré-Columbiana," *A União* 18 (1969).
"The Metcalf Stone," *Manuscripts* 21 (1969): 159–68.
"Ontdekten de Foeniciers Amerika," *Spiegel Historiael* 4 (1969): 323–29.
Preface to *The Key,* by J. P. Cohane. New York: Crown Publishers, 1969.

"Semites Discovered America 3000 Years Ago," *Hadassah* 17 (1969): 35–38.

"Toward a History of Ancient America," *Dialogue* 4 (2, 1969): 64–71.

"Near East Contact With Ancient America," *Institute of Religion* (October 9, 1970): 1–8.

"America and the Ecumene of the Old Testament," *Newsletter and Proceedings of the Society for Early Historic Archaeology* 125 (1971): 1–10.

"America and the Ecumene of the Old Testament (Illustrated ed.)," *Ensign* 1 (1971).

"The Bat Creek Inscription," *Argosy* (January 1971): 24–27.

"Did Semites Beat Columbus to America?" *Jewish Digest* 16 (8, 1971): 28–30.

"The Metcalf Stone," *Explorers Journal* 49 (1971): 176–80. Rev. repr. of *Manuscripts* 21 (1969): 159–68.

"Pre-Columbian Discoveries Link Old and New Worlds," *Ensign* (October 1971): 56–63.

"Before Columbus and the Vikings," *The American Zionist* 63 (1972): 22–25.

"Riddles of the Wise," *Berytus* 21 (1972): 17–33.

"A Hebrew Inscription Authenticated." Pages 67–80 in vol. 1 of *Essays in Honor of Hugh W. Nibley on the Occasion of His Eightieth Birthday, 27 March 1990: By Study and Also by Faith*. Ed. J. M. Lundquist and S. D. Ricks. Salt Lake City: Deseret Book Company, 1990.

"A Hebrew Inscription Authenticated (reprint)," *Louisiana Mounds Society* 39–42 (1991): 5–6, 4–5, 7, 8–9.

"The Hebrew Presence in Pre-Columbian America," *New England Antiquities Research Association* 27 (3–4, 1991): 91–95.

"New Directions in the Study of Ancient Middle Eastern Cultures." Pages 53–65 in *Bulletin of the Middle Eastern Culture Center in Japan. V. Near Eastern Studies: Dedicated to H. I. H. Prince Takahito Mikasa on the Occasion of His Seventy-Fifth Birthday*. Ed. M. Mori. Wiesbaden: Otto Harrassowitz, 1991.

"Burrows' Cave: Fact or Fiction?" *Louisiana Mounds Society Newsletter* (1992): 6–7.

"The Ten Lost Tribes." Pages 61–69 in *Hebrew and the Bible in America: The First Two Centuries*. Ed. Shalom Goldman. Hanover: University Press of New England, 1993.

"The Background to Jewish Studies in the Bible and in the Ancient East," *Shofar* 12 (4, 1994): 1–46.

"Diffusion of Near East Culture in Antiquity and in Byzantine Times," *Orient* 30–31 (1995): 69–81.

"The Near East Background of the Rigveda." Pages 117–20 in *Ancient Egyptian and Mediterranean Studies in Memory of William A. Ward*. Ed. L. Lesko. Providence: Dept. of Egyptology, Brown University, 1998.

Collaborative Work

Srinivasan, L., and C. H. Gordon. "Canaanite Vocabulary in Bengali and in Some Other IE Dialects of India," *Mother Tongue* 1 (1995): 202–6.

Review

Jairazbhoy, R. A. *Ancient Egyptians and Chinese in America. Archaeological News* 4 (2–3, 1975): 58–59.

Mediterranean Studies

Articles

"Vergil and the Near East," *Ugaritica, Dedicated to C. Schaeffer* 6 (1969): 267–88.

"East Mediterranean Synthesis." Pages 188–96 in *The Crisis Years: The 12th Century BCE: From the Danube to the Tigris*. Dubuque: Kendall/Hunt, 1990.

Review

Butterworth, E. A. S. *The Tree at the Navel of the Earth. Bulletin of the School of Oriental (and African) Studies* 34 (1971).

Miscellaneous

Article

"A Letter." Pages 92–93 in *Famous Ways to Grow Old*. Ed. P. Bristow. London: Age Concern, 1989.

Minoan

Books

Evidence for the Minoan Language. Ventnor, N.J.: Ventnor Publishers, 1966.
Ugarit and Minoan Crete. New York: W. W. Norton, 1966.

Articles

"Akkadian Tablets in Minoan Dress," *Antiquity* 31 (1957): 237–40.
"Notes on Linear A," *Antiquity* 31 (1957): 124–30.
"Minoan Linear A," *Journal of Near Eastern Studies* 17 (1958): 245–55.
"Re: Minoan," *Antiquity* 32 (1958): 215–16.
"Labyrinthine Ways," Letter to the editor of the *Washington Post* (June 1959).
"The Language of the Hagia Triada Tablets." Third International Congress of Classical Studies. *Nestor* 70 (1959).
"The Language of the Hagia Triada Tablets," *Klio* (1960): 63–68.

"Eteocretan." Newsletter distributed by the author, 1962.
"Eteocretan and Minoan." Newsletter distributed by the author, 1962.
"Minoan." Newsletter distributed by the author, 1962.
"Minoica," *Journal of Near Eastern Studies* 21 (1962): 207–10.
"To My Students." Newsletter distributed by the author, 1962.
"The Decipherment of Minoan," *Natural History* 72 (November 1963): 22–31.
"The Development of the Alphabet on Crete," *The Classical World* 57 (December 1963): 99–100.
"The Dreros Bilingual," *Journal of Semitic Studies* 8 (1963): 76–79.
"The Minoan Bridge: Newest Frontier in Biblical Studies," *Christianity Today* 7 (March 15, 1963): 3–8.
"Minoan Civilization." Pages 330–35 in vol. 16 of *Colliers Encyclopedia*. New York: Colliers, 1963.
"The Minoan Cult," *Nestor* 2 (1963): 235.
"תחום חדש לקדמניות השמיות (A New Province of Semitic Antiquity)." Pages 13–16 in *Oz l-David*. David Ben-Gurion Festschrift. Jerusalem: Magnes Press, 1963.
"Toward a Grammar of Minoan," *Orientalia* 32 (1963): 292–97.
"Worksheets on Greco-Semitic Bilinguals." Newsletter distributed by the author, 1963.
"Notes on Linear A." Pages 183–86 in *Mycenaean Studies*. Ed. J. Emmett and L. Bennett. Madison: University of Wisconsin Press, 1964.
"Linguistic Continuity From Minoan to Eteocretan," *Studi Micenei ed Egeo-Anatolici* (1967): 89–92.
"The Present Status of Minoan Studies." In *Atti e Memorie del I⁰ Congresso Internazionale de Micenologia*. Rome: Edizione dell'Ateneo, 1967.
"Crete in the Ugaritic Tablets." In *Second International Cretological Congress*. Athens: Hellenic Society for Humanistic Studies, 1968.
"*Ki–de–ma–we–re* (HT 31:4)," *Kadmos* 8 (2, 1969): 131–33.
"Minoan." Pages 125–35 in *Studi in Onore de Piero Meriggi = Athenaeum* NS 47 (1969).
"Greek and Eteocretan Unilinguals From Praisos and Dreros," *Berytus* 19 (1970): 95–98.
"In the Wake of Minoan and Eteocretan." Pages 164–71 in *First International Cretological Congress at Delphi*. Athens: Hellenic Society for Humanistic Studies, 1970.
"*Mi–ru–su–ra–re* (HT 117:a:4–5)," *Studi Micenei ed Egeo–Anatolici* 11 (1970): 58–59.
"The Greek Unilinguals From Praisos and Dreros and Their Bearing on Eteocretan and Minoan." Pages 97–103 in *International Conference of Cretologists*. Athens: Hellenic Society for Humanistic Studies, 1971.

"The Language of Crete: A New Area for the Science of the Hebrew Language." Pages 186–239 in vol. 1 of *Hagut Ivrit b-Amerika*. Ed. M. Zohari, A. Tartakover, and H. Ormian. Tel Aviv: Yavneh, 1972.

"The Minoan Connection," *Natural History* 81 (8, 1972): 74–84.

"Nero's Estimate of Minoan." Pages 593–605 in *Estratto da Studi in Onore de Eduardo Volterra*. Rome: Giuffrè Editore, 1972.

"In the Wake of Minoan and Eteocretan." Pages 163–71 and plates I–IV in *Proceedings of the First International Humanistic Symposium at Delphi*. Athens: Hellenic Society for Humanistic Studies, 1973.

"The Decipherment of Minoan and Eteocretan," *Journal of the Royal Asiatic Society* (1975): 148–58.

"Further Notes on the Hagia Triada Tablet No. 31," *Kadmos* 15 (1976): 28–30.

"Ebla and the Minoan Problem." Pages 209–12 in vol. 1 of *Studia Mediterranea: Piero Meriggi dicata*. Ed. O. Carruba. Pavia, 1979.

"The Semitic Language of Minoan Crete." Pages 763–82 in *Amsterdam Studies in the Theory and History of Linguistic Science. IV. Current Issues in Linguistic Theory = Bono Homini Donum: Essays in Historical Linguistics, in Memory of J. Alexander Kerns*. Amsterdam: John Benjamins, 1979.

"New Light on the Minoan Language." In *Fourth International Cretological Congress*. Ed. Y. L. Arbeitman and A. R. Bomhard. Athens: Hellenic Society for Humanistic Studies, 1980.

"Reflections on the Decipherment of Minoan," *Orientalia* 53 (1984): 453–55.

"Semitic Inscriptions From Crete." Pages 83–88 in *Hebrew Annual Review: Biblical and Other Studies in Honor of Sheldon H. Blank*. Ed. R. Ahroni. Ohio: Ohio State University Press, 1984.

"A Recent Attempt to Decipher Linear A and the Phaistos Disc," *Orientalia* (1990).

"New Directions in the Study of Ancient Middle Eastern Cultures." Pages 53–65 in *Bulletin of the Middle Eastern Culture Center in Japan. V. Near Eastern Studies: Dedicated to H. I. H. Prince Takahito Mikasa on the Occasion of His Seventy-Fifth Birthday*. Ed. M. Mori. Wiesbaden: Otto Harrassowitz, 1991.

"Minoan Civilization." Pages 330–36 in *Colliers Encyclopedia*. New York: Colliers, 1995.

Reviews

Bernal, M. *Black Athena. Journal of the American Oriental Society* 113 (1993): 489–90.

Palmer, L. R., and J. Chadwick, eds. *Proceedings of the Cambridge Colloquium on Mycenaean Studies. American Historical Review* 73 (1967): 108–9.

Toynbee, A. "Some Problems of Greek History." *The Annals of The American Academy of Political and Social Science* 391 (September 1970): 207–8.

Nuzi

Book

Nouns in the Nuzi Tablets. Babyloniaca 16. Paris: Paul Geuthner, 1936.

Articles

"The Names of the Months in the Nuzi Calendar," *Revista degli studi orentali* 15 (1934): 253–57.
"Numerals in the Nuzi Tablets," *Revue d'Assyriologie* 31 (1934): 53–60.
"Points of the Compass in the Nuzi Tablets," *Revue d'Assyriologie* 31 (1934): 101–8.
"The Pronoun in the Nuzi Tablets," *American Journal of Semitic Languages* 51 (1934): 1–21.
"Fifteen Nuzi Tablets Relating to Women," *Le Muséon* 48 (1935): 113–32.
"Nuzi Tablets Relating to Women," *Analecta Orientalia (Dedicated to Antonio Deimel)* 12 (1935): 163–84.
"Parallèles Nouziens aux lois et coûtumes de l'Ancien Testament," *Revue Biblique* 44 (1935): 34–41.
"Evidence for the Horite Language From Nuzi," *Bulletin of the American Schools of Oriental Research* 64 (1936): 23–28.
"Nuzi Tablets Relating to Theft," *Orientalia* 5 (1936): 305–30.
"The Status of Women Reflected in the Nuzi Tablets," *Zeitschrift für Assyriologie* 43 (1936): 146–69.
"The Story of Jacob and Laban in the Light of the Nuzi Tablets," *Bulletin of the American Schools of Oriental Research* 66 (1937): 25–27.
"The Dialact of the Nuzu Tablets," *Orientalia* 7 (1938): 1–50.
"The People Versus the Mayor," *Smith Alumnae Quarterly* (August 1941): 227–28.
"The Glyptic Art of Nuzu," *Journal of Near Eastern Studies* 7 (1948): 261–66.
"Erebu Marriage." Pages 155–60 in *Civilization and Culture of Nuzi and the Hurrians, in Honor of Ernest R. Lacheman*. Ed. M. A. Morrison and D. I. Owen. Winona Lake, Ind.: Eisenbrauns, 1981.
"In Memoriam: Ernest Lacheman," *Orientalia* 52 (1983): 426–28.

Collaborative Work

Gordon, C. H., and E. R. Lacheman. "The Nuzu Menology," *Archiv Orientální* 10 (1938): 51–64.

Reviews

Lacheman, E. R. *Miscellaneous Texts from Nuzi. II. The Palace and Temple Archives. Orientalia* 21 (1952): 373–81.

Saarisalo, A. *New Kirkuk Documents Relating to Slaves.* Studia orientalia 5. *Journal of the Palestine Oriental Society* 15 (1935): 349–50.

Phoenician and Hebrew Inscriptions

Articles

"Lachish Letter IV," *Bulletin of the American Schools of Oriental Research* 67 (1937): 30–32.

"Notes on the Lachish Letters," *Bulletin of the American Schools of Oriental Research* 70 (1938): 17–18.

"Two Northwest-Semitic Inscriptions From Tarsus," *Bulletin of the American Schools of Oriental Research* 78 (1940): 9–11.

"Phoenician Inscriptions From Karatepe," *Jewish Quarterly Review* NS 39 (1948): 41–50.

"Azitawadd's Phoenician Inscription," *Journal of Near Eastern Studies* 8 (1949): 108–15.

"Northwest Semitic Texts in Latin and Greek Letters," *Journal of the American Oriental Society* 88 (1968): 285–89.

Reviews

Friedrich, J. *Phönizisch-punische Grammatik.* Orientalia 21 (1952): 119–23.

Obermann, J. *Discoveries at Karatepe: A Phoenician Royal Inscription From Cilicia.BASOR* 110 (1948): 193–96.

Sznycer, M. *Les passages puniques en transcription latine dans le "Poenulus" de Plaute.* Etudes et Commentaires 65. *Journal of the American Oriental Society* 89 (1969): 182–83.

Scripts and Their Decipherment

Books

Forgotten Scripts: How They Were Deciphered and Their Impact on Contemporary Culture. New York: Basic Books, 1968.

Forgotten Scripts: The Story of Their Decipherment. London: Thames and Hudson, 1968.

Scritture Dimenticate. Rome: Casa Editrice Astrolabio, 1969. Italians trans. of *Forgotten Scripts.*

Forgotten Scripts. Harmondsworth: Penguin Books, 1971.

Kodai-Moji-no-Nazo: Oriento-shogo no Kaidoku. Tokyo: Shakai-Shiso-sha, 1971. Japanese trans. of *Forgotten Scripts.*

Forgotten Scripts: Their Ongoing Discovery and Decipherment. New York: Basic Books, 1982.

Articles

"The Recovery of Lost Languages," *Medical Opinion and Review* 4 (4, 1968): 36–55.

"El Rescate de Lenguas Perdidas," *Estudios Orientales* 4 (1, 1969): 28–40.

"The Accidental Invention of the Phonemic Alphabet," *Journal of Near Eastern Studies* 29 (1970): 193–97.

"The Alphabet," *New York University Educational Quarterly* 5 (4, 1974): 11–15.

"The Alphabet," *New England Social Studies Bulletin* 36 (1, 1978): 18–25.

"Cracking the Code," *Odyssey* (1980): 53–54.

Reviews

Diringer, D. *The Alphabet: A Key to the History of Mankind, "Starting at 'A'". The Washington Post BOOK WORLD* 3 (1969): 10.

———. *Writing. Archaeology* (Spring 1963).

Friedrich, J. *Extinct Languages. Journal of Bible and Religion* 15 (1957): 34–35.

Grimme, H. *Altsinaitische Forschungen: Epigraphisches und Historisches.* Studien zur Geschichte und Kultur des Altertums 20. *Orientalia* 8 (1939): 177–78.

Jensen, H. *Sign, Symbol and Script: An Account of Man's Efforts to Write. Boston Sunday Herald Traveler Book Guide* (March 1, 1970): 1–2.

Kahn, D. *The Codebreakers: The Story of Secret Writing. The Annals of the American Academy* (January 1968): 240–41.

Ugarit

Books

Ugaritic Grammar. Rome: Pontifical Biblical Institute, 1940.

The Loves and Wars of Baal and Anat. Princeton: Princeton University Press. 1943.

Ugaritic Handbook. Rome: Pontifical Biblical Institute, 1947.

Ugaritic Literature: A Comprehensive Translation of the Poetic and Prose Texts. Rome: Pontifical Biblical Institute. 1949.

Ugaritic Manual. Rome: Pontifical Biblical Institute, 1955.

Ugaritic Textbook. Rome: Pontifical Biblical Institute, 1965.

Ugarit and Minoan Crete. New York: W. W. Norton, 1966.

Ugaritic Textbook. Rome: Pontifical Biblical Institute, 1967.

Ugaritic Textbook. Rev. repr. Rome: Pontifical Biblical Institute, 1998.

Articles

"A Marriage of the Gods in Canaanite Mythology," *Bulletin of the American Schools of Oriental Research* 65 (1937): 29–33.

"*Trh, ṯn*, and *nkr* in the Ras Shamra Tablets," *Journal of Biblical Literature* 57 (1938): 407–10.

"ספורי המקרא לאור החפירות (Biblical Narratives in the Light of Archaeology," *Bitzaron* 3 (3, 1940): 162–71.

"The Daughters of Baal and Allah," *The Moslem World* 33 (1, 1943): 50–51.

"The Poetic Literature of Ugarit," *Orientalia* 12 (1943): 31–75.

"The Ugaritic 'ABC'," *Orientalia* 19 (1950): 374–76.

"Ugaritica," *Journal of Near Eastern Studies* 9 (1950): 78–81.

"Notes on the Legend of Keret," *Journal of Near Eastern Studies* 11 (1952): 212–13.

"Ugarit As Link Between Greek and Hebrew Literatures," *Revista degli studi orientali* 29 (1954): 161–69.

"Ugarit and Caphtor," *Minos* 3 (2, 1955): 126–32.

"Observations on the Akkadian Tablets From Ugarit," *Revue d'Assyriologie* 50 (1956): 127–33.

"Ugaritic Guilds and Homeric Demioergoi." Pages 136–43 in *The Aegean and Near East Studies Presented to Hetty Goldman*. Locust Valley, N.Y.: J. J. Agustin, 1956.

"Ugaritic *hrt/hiritu* 'Cemetery'," *Syria* 33 (1956): 102–3.

"Canaanite Mythology." Pages 183–217 in *Mythologies of the Ancient World*. Ed. S. N. Kramer. Garden City, N.Y.: Doubleday, 1961.

"New Data on Ugaritic Numerals." Pages 127–30 in *Studia Ioanni Bakos Dicata*. Bratislava, 1965.

"Crete in the Ugaritic Tablets." In *Second International Cretological Congress*. Athens: Hellenic Society for Humanistic Studies, 1968.

"Vergil and the Near East," *Ugaritica, Dedicated to C. Schaeffer* 6 (1969): 267–88.

"Baal." In *Encyclopaedia Britannica*. 15th ed. Chicago, 1974.

"Ugarit and Its Significance," *Arts, The Journal of the Sydney University Arts Association* 9 (1974): 22–29.

"Ugarit and Its Significance to Biblical Studies." Pages 161–69 in *Biblical Studies in Contemporary Thought*. Ed. M. Ward. Burlington, Vt.: Trinity College Biblical Institute, 1975.

"El, Father of Šnm," *Journal of Near Eastern Studies* 35 (1976): 261–62.

"Poetic Legends and Myths From Ugarit," *Berytus* 25 (1977): 5–133.

"Ebla and the Minoan Problem." Pages 209–12 in vol. 1 of *Studia Mediterranea: Piero Meriggi dicata*. Ed. O. Carruba. Pavia, 1979.

"Eblaite and Its Affinities." Pages 297–301 in *Amsterdam Studies in the Theory and History of Linguistic Science*. IV. *Current Issues in Linguistic Theory*. Oswald Szemerényi Festschrist. Amsterdam: John Benjamins, 1979.

"Echoes of Ebla." Pages 133–39 in *Essays on the Occasion of the Seventieth Anniversary of The Dropsie University*. Philadelphia: Dropsie University Press, 1979.

"An Inventory of Instruments From the Bronze Age," *Revista da Universidadede Coimbra* 27 (1979): 141–45.

"The Seventh Day," *Ugarit-Forschungen* 11 (1979): 299–301.

"לוחות אבלה ועולם המקרא" (The Ebla Tablets and the Biblical World)," *Bitzaron* 3 NS 9–10 (1981): 17–26.

"Philology, Lexical Notes," *Newsletter for Ugaritic Studies* (1981): 9–10.

"Ugarit in Retrospect and Prospect." Pages 183–89 in *Ugarit in Retrospect: Fifty Years of Ugarit and Ugaritic, in Honor of Claude Schaeffer*. Ed. G. D. Young. Winona Lake, Ind.: Eisenbrauns, 1981.

"Ugaritic *ik* 'How?'," *Newsletter for Ugaritic Studies* 26 (1981): 9–10.

"The Three Graces," *Newsletter for Ugaritic Studies* 31 (1984): 11.

"The Devil, HBY," *Newsletter for Ugaritic Studies* 33 (1985): 15.

"The Ugaritic Texts: Half a Century of Research." In *Biblical Archaeology Today*. Jerusalem: Israel Exploration Society; The Israel Academy of Sciences and Humanities in cooperation with American Schools of Oriental Research, 1985.

"Ḥ̄BY, Possessor of Horns and Tail," *Ugarit-Forschungen* 18 (1987): 129–32.

"כתבי אוגריתית—50 שנות החקר" (A Half Century of Ugaritic Research)," *Bitzaron* 8 NS 32–33 (1987): 20–29.

"Marriage in the Guise of Siblingship," *Ugarit-Forschungen* 20 (1988): 53–56.

"Ugaritic RBT / RABITU." Pages 127–32 in *Ascribe to the Lord: Biblical and Other Studies in Memory of Peter C. Craigie*. Journal for the Study of the Old Testament: Supplement Series 67. Ed. L. Eslinger and G. Taylor. Sheffield: JSOT, 1988.

"Ebla, Ugarit and the Old Testament," *Orient* 25 (1989): 134–68.

"In Memoriam: Claude Frederic Armand Schaeffer (1898–1982)." Pages 141–44 in vol. 2 of *Eblaitica: Essays on the Ebla Archives and Eblaite Language*. Ed. C. H. Gordon and G. A. Rendsburg. Winona Lake, Ind.: Eisenbrauns, 1990.

"A Response to W. G. Lambert." Pages 145–46 in vol. 2 of *Eblaitica: Essays on the Ebla Archives and Eblaite Language*. Ed. C. H. Gordon and G. A. Rendsburg. Winona Lake, Ind.: Eisenbrauns, 1990.

"נישואים במסווה של אחים ואחיות," *Bitzaron* 10 NS The Jubilee Issue (1990): 147–49.

"Ugarit and the Old Testament (in Korean)," 1990.

"The Background to Jewish Studies in the Bible and in the Ancient East," *Shofar* 12 (4, 1994): 1–46.

"Sixty Years in Ugaritology." In *Le pays d'Ougarit autour de 1200 av. 1200 av. J.-C.* Ras Shamra-Ougarit 11. Paris: Editions Recherche sur les Civilisations, 1995.

"Ugaritic Phonology." Pages 49–54 in *Phonologies of Asia and Africa (Including the Caucasus)*. Ed. Alan S. Kaye. Winona Lake, Ind.: Eisenbrauns, 1997.

Reviews

Aistleitner, J. *Untersuchen zur Grammatik des Ugaritischen.* Orientalia 25 (1956): 110–12.

Cassuto, U. *The Goddess Anath: Canaanite Epics of the Patriarchal Age: Texts, Hebrew Translation, Commentary and Introduction. Journal of the American Oriental Society* 72 (1952): 180–81.

Fronzaroli, P. La Fonetica Ugaritica. Orientalia 25 (1956): 433–34.

———. *Leggenda di Aqat. Journal of Near Eastern Studies* 17 (1958): 86.

Ginzberg, H. L. *The Legend of Keret: A Canaanite Epic of the Bronze Age.* Bulletin of the American Schools of Oriental Research 105 (1947): 11–12.

Gray, J. *The Krt Text in the Literature of Ras Shamra: A Social Myth of Ancient Canaan. Journal of Near Eastern Studies* 17 (1958): 86–87.

Herdner, A. *Corpus des tablettes en cunéiforme alphabétique. Journal of Near Eastern Studies* 25 (1966): 63–65.

Kapelrud, A. S. *Baal in the Ras Shamra Texts. Antiquity* 111 (1954): 186–88.

———. *The Ras Shamra Discoveries and the Old Testament. Jewish Social Studies* 27 (1965): 112.

———. "Ras Sjamra-Funenne og det Gamle Testamentet." *Journal of Biblical Literature* 74 (1955): 292–93.

Langhe, R. de. *Les textes de Ras Shamra et leurs Rapports avec le milieu biblique de l'Ancient Testament. Journal of Biblical Literature* 66 (1947): 248.

Largement, R. *La Naissance de l'Aurore: Poème de Ras Shamra-Ugarit. Journal of Near Eastern Studies* 11 (1952): 144.

Liverani, M. *Storia de Ugarit: Nell' età degli archivi politici. Journal of Semitic Studies* 9 (1964): 363–64.

Obermann, J. Ugaritic Mythology. *Crozer Quarterly* 25 (1948): 269–71.

———. *Ugaritic Mythology.* Orientalia 17 (1948): 121–22.

———. *How Daniel Was Blessed With a Son: An Incubation Scene in Ugaritic. Journal of Biblical Literature* 66 (1947): 248–49.

Rin, S. *Acts of the Gods: The Ugaritic Epic Poetry. Jewish Social Studies* 31 (1, 1969): 48.

Segert, S. *A Basic Grammar of the Ugaritic Language: With Selected Texts and Glossary. Journal of Biblical Literature* 106 (1987): 113–14.

Selms, A. von. *Marriage and Family Life in Ugaritic Literature.* Orientalia 24 (1955): 327–29.

Virolleaud, C. *Le palais royal d'Ugarit V. Journal of Semitic Studies* 12 (1967): 110–11.

INDEX

Ader 41–42
Adler, Cyrus 79 n. 26, 81–82, 82 n. 29
Albright, William F. 23 n. 9, 25–26, 25 n. 10, 27, 38–39, 38 n. 20, 41, 42–43, 46, 40, 49, 50–51, 53, 03, 84, 93, 104
American Academy of Arts and Sciences 53, 92
American Schools of Oriental Research 16 n. 2, 17 n. 4, 22, 22 n. 9, 25–26, 27, 40, 42–43, 44, 48, 102
Aramaic magic bowls 23–24, 25, 30–31, 37
Avi-Yonah, Michael 31
Bache, Charles 34, 46, 48
Balmuth, Miriam 93, 93 n. 36
Barton, George Aaron 17–18, 17 n. 4, 23 n. 9
Beidler, Paul 35
Bender, Harold 58
Beth-Sur 23, 26, 27, 30, 40
Bialik, Hayyim Nahman 30
Bonfante, Giuliano 82–83
Brandeis University 84–90, 85 n. 31, 89 n. 34, 93, 94, 95, 96–100, 101, 108
Brown, W. Norman 111
Chow, Wilson 99
Contenau, Georges 38
Conway, Agnes 46
Cooper, Jerrold S. 48
Crown, Alan 100
cryptanalysis 61–63
Dartmouth College 95, 108
Dead Sea Scrolls 79 n. 27, 85
Deimel, Anton 19, 19 n. 6
Dhorme, Édouard 20
Documentary Hypothesis 80–81
Dörpfeld, Wilhelm 27
Dow, Sterling 57–58
Dropsie College 3, 17, 18 n. 5, 20, 20 n. 8, 34 n. 16, 75, 79–84, 79, n. 26, 82 n. 29, 96
Dussaud, René 38
Ebla 101, 104–5, 105 n. 40, 107
École Biblique 29, 30
Edgerton, Harold 89–90
Edgerton, William 84
Edom 44–47
Einstein, Albert 2–3, 56
Epstein, Yitshaq 40
Fein, Jack 91–92
Fiore, Silvestro 95, 96
Fisher, Clarence S. 23 n. 9, 26
Fisher, Loren R. 96
Fuller, Anne H. 42–43
Gadalla, Fawzi Fahim 87
Garrod, Dorothy 87
Gehman, Henry S. 82
Ginsberg, H. L. 51, 51 n. 22, 56
global diffusion 1–2, 94–95, 108, 109–13
Glueck, Nelson 39, 39 n. 20, 44–47
Goldman, Shalom 101, 108
Goodenough, Erwin 95, 98–99
Gordon, Constance V. 104, 107–8, 111, 113
Gottlieb, Claire 101, 102, 103, 103 n. 39
Gratz College 14
Graves, Robert 93–94
Grossberg, Daniel 101, 104
Hamadan 73, 74
Hanfmann, George 93
Harris, Zelig 21
Herzfeld, Ernst 54, 55, 56, 72
Hitti, Philip K. 82
Hoffner, Harry 87
Hopkins, David 103
Horsefield, George 46
Hoshander, Jacob 15
Institute for Advanced Study 3, 53, 54, 55, 57, 82

Isfahan 73, 74
Jacobs, Maurice 84
Johns Hopkins University 25 n. 10, 26 n. 12, 39 n. 20, 48, 49, 53, 56, 81–82, 82 n. 29, 93
Keller, Sharon 101, 102, 103 n. 39
Kent, Roland G. 58, 58 n. 23, 67
Kenyon, Kathleen 23 n. 9
Khorsabad 34–35
Kramer, Samuel N. 18, 18 n. 5, 83
Lacheman, Ernest R. 95, 98, 99
Lagrange, Marie-Joseph 29–30, 30 n. 14
Lasor, William Sanford 79, 79 n. 27
Lauer, J. P. 66
Lee, Jin Tai/Tae?? 108
Leslau, Wolf 84
Lewisohn, Ludwig 84
Lewy, Julius 38
Linder, Elisha 89, 90–91, 108
Loud, Gordon 34
Lubetski, Meir 101, 102, 103, 103 n. 29
Mair, Victor 109, 111
Malek-esh-Sho'ara 71–72
Margolis, Max 17, 20, 20 n. 8, 21, 34 n. 16, 79, 103
Mari 36, 36 n. 18
Megiddo 29
Mendelsohn, Isaac 89
Metzger, Bruce 82, 82 n. 30
Mikasa, Takahito 99, 107, 108
Minoan Linear A 48, 49–50, 62, 85 n. 31, 88, 88 n. 33, 90, 92
Moab 41–42, 44–45, 47
Montgomery, James A. 15, 16, 16 n. 2, 17, 19, 22, 23, 24, 30, 34 n. 16, 44, 103, 111
Morrison, Martha 86, 95
mullahs 69–70
Nabatea 39 n. 20, 46
Negev 39 n. 20, 44, 47
Neuman, Abraham A. 81–82
New York University 86, 100–104, 107, 108, 111
Nippur 23, 23 n. 9, 24

Nuzi 34 n. 16, 36, 37–38, 86, 95
Olmstead, A. T. 57–58
Oriental Institute of the University of Chicago 18, 18 n. 5, 42, 57, 84, 87, 97
Owen, David 86
Parrot, André 36, 36 n. 18
Parthenon 25, 75
Petra 46
Petrie, William Matthew Flinders 23 n. 9, 27–29, 27 n. 13
Pohl, Alfredo 20, 20 n. 7
Pontifical Biblical Institute 19, 19 n. 6, 20 n. 7, 30, 56, 97
Pontificium Institutum Biblicum see Pontifical Biblical Institute
Poebel, Arno 18
Radovsky, David 100
Redfield, Robert 42, 43
Redner, Harry 100
Reich, Nathaniel 83
Reischauer, Edwin 62
Reisner, George A. 23 n. 9
Rendsburg, Gary 101
Robinson, David 93
Robinson, James 96, 96 n. 38
Rodin, Judith 103–4
Rose, David 104
Rossell, William 80
Rothenburg, Benno 47
Royal Asiatic Society 92
Sachar, Abram 84, 84, 88, 89, 89 n. 34, 89 n. 35
Sasson, Jack 86–87
Sbeita 47
Schliemann, Heinrich 27, 90
Segal, Nelly 111, 112
Sellers, Ovid R. 26
Shibaniba see Tell Billa
Shiraz 73, 74
Sinai 44
Skoss, Solomon 17
Smith College 51, 53–54, 59
Society for Near Eastern Studies 107
Society of Biblical Literature 16 n. 2, 20 n. 8, 23 n. 9, 26, 102

Spanier, Ktziah 101
Speiser, Ephraim A. 17, 18 n. 5, 33, 34, 34 n. 16, 44, 48, 53
Srinivasan, Liny 112
Steindorff, Georg 50
Steinspring, William 43
Stendahl, Krister 57
Talmud 5–6, 8, 14, 15, 17
Tell Atchana 35 n. 17
Tell Beit Mirsim 26, 38, 39, 39 n. 20, 40
Tell Billa 23, 33, 40, 44, 47
Tell el-ʿAjjūl 28
Tell el-Hesi 23 n. 9, 27
Tepe Gawra 23, 33, 34, 41, 44, 47
Thureau-Dangin, François 38
Tsumura, David Toshio 99, 107
Ugarit/Ugaritic 17, 20, 38, 38 n. 19, 48, 49, 50, 51 n. 22, 54, 55, 56–57, 58, 61, 79, 80, 88, 91, 92, 93, 104, 109–10, 112
Uppvall, Axel Johann 18
University of Haifa 91, 108
Univeristy of Pennsylvania 15, 16, 16 nn. 1–2, 17, 17 n. 4, 18 n. 5, 19, 20, 21, 23, 23 n. 9, 24, 30, 34, 34 n. 16, 55, 58 n. 23, 82 n. 29, 103, 109, 111

Ur (Sumer) 35–36, 35 n. 17
Ventris, Michael 88, 88 n. 32
Virolleaud, Charles 38, 38 n. 19
Wallace, Constance V.
  see Gordon, Constance V.
Ward, William A. 96, 112 n. 42
Weeks, Noel 100
Weisskopf, Victor 92–93
Wesselhoeft, E. C. 18
Wheeler, Mortimer 23 n. 9
Wolfson, Harry 5–6
Woolley, C. Leonard 35–36, 35 n. 17
Worrell, William 84
Wright, G. Ernest 23 n. 9, 39, 39 n. 20
Yamauchi, Edwin 98
Yeivin, Samuel 28–29
Yellin, David 40
Young, Dwight 84
Young, Fred 80
Young, G. Douglas 79, 79 n. 27
Žabkar, Louis Vico 95, 97–98, 99
Zeitlin, Solomon 17

SOCIETY OF BIBLICAL LITERATURE
BIBLICAL SCHOLARSHIP IN NORTH AMERICA

Kent Harold Richards, Editor

Frank Chamberlain Porter: Pioneer in American Biblical Interpretation	Roy A. Harrisville
Benjamin Wisner Bacon: Pioneer in American Biblical Criticism	Roy A. Harrisville
A Fragile Craft: The Work of Amos Niven Wilder	John Dominic Crossan
Edgar Johnson Goodspeed: Articulate Scholar	James Cook
Shirley Jackson Case and the Chicago School: The Socio-Historical Method	William J. Hynes
Humanizing America's Iconic Book	Gene M. Tucker and Douglas A. Knight, editors
A History of Biblical Studies in Canada: A Sense of Proportion	John S. Moir
Searching the Scriptures: A History of the Society of Biblical Literature, 1880-1980	Ernest W. Saunders
Horace Bushnell: On the Vitality of Biblical Language	James O. Duke
Feminist Perspectives on Biblical Scholarship	Adela Yarbro Collins, editor
Erwin Ramsdell Goodenough: A Personal Pilgrimage	Robert S. Eccles
A Century of Greco-Roman Philology: Featuring the American Philological Association and the Society of Biblical Literature	Frederick William Danker
The Pennsylvania Tradition of Semitics: A Century of Near Eastern and Biblical Studies at the University of Pennsylvania	Cyrus Gordon
Moses Stuart	John H. Giltner
Max Leopold Margolis: A Scholar's Scholar	Leonard Greenspoon
The Bible and the University: The Messianic Vision of William Rainey Harper	James P. Wind
A History of Bible Translation and the North American Contribution	Harry M. Orlinsky and Robert G. Bratcher
Cadbury, Knox, and Talbert: American Contributions to the Study of Acts	Mikeal C. Parsons and Joseph B. Tyson, editors
The Times and Life of Edward Robinson: Connecticut Yankee in King Solomon's Court	Jay G. Williams
A Scholar's Odyssey	Cyrus H. Gordon